THE MEN
IN WHITE

Also by Anosh Irani

THE MEN
IN WHITE

ANOSH IRANI

ANANSI

Published in Canada in 2018 and the USA in 2019 by House of Anansi Press Inc.
www.houseofanansi.com

House of Anansi Press is committed to protecting our natural environment.
As part of our efforts, the interior of this book is printed on paper that contains 100%
post-consumer recycled fibres, is acid-free, and is processed chlorine-free.

22 21 20 19 18   1 2 3 4 5

Library and Archives Canada Cataloguing in Publication

Irani, Anosh, 1974–, author
The men in white / Anosh Irani.
A play.

Issued in print and electronic formats.

ISBN 978-1-4870-0473-6 (softcover).—ISBN 978-1-4870-0474-3 (EPUB).—
ISBN 978-1-4870-0475-0 (Kindle)

I. Title.

PS8617.R36M46 2018   C812'.6   C2018-900718-4
                                             C2018-900719-2

Library of Congress Control Number: 2018949216

Cover image: Boman Irani
Photographs on pp. xi and xii: Emily Cooper

Text design and typesetting: Laura Brady

*We acknowledge for their financial support of our publishing program the Canada Council
for the Arts, the Ontario Arts Council, and the Government of Canada.*

Printed and bound in Canada

For Iris

The Men in White made its debut at the Arts Club Theatre Company's Granville Island Stage, in Vancouver, British Columbia, where it was first performed on February 15, 2017. The play received its Toronto premiere at the Factory Theatre on October 18, 2018. The original cast members and creative team are:

Cast

BABA	Sanjay Talwar
HASAN	Nadeem Phillip
HASEENA	Risha Nanda
ABDUL	Shekhar Paleja
DOC	Munish Sharma
RAM	Anousha Alamian
RANDY	Parm Soor
SAM	Raugi Yu
TONY	Kamyar Pazandeh (Arts Club Theatre production)

Creative Team

DIRECTOR/ DRAMATURG	Rachel Ditor
SET DESIGNER	Amir Ofek
LIGHTING DESIGNER	Adrian Muir
SOUND DESIGNER	Murray Price
COSTUME DESIGNER	Amy McDougall
STAGE MANAGER	Caryn Fehr
ASSISTANT STAGE MANAGER	Ronaye Haynes
ASSISTANT TO THE DIRECTOR	Gavan Cheema

CHARACTERS

MUMBAI

BABA
Late 60s. Owner of a chicken slaughterhouse.

HASAN
Eighteen years old. Madly, passionately in love with cricket. Expert chicken cutter as well. Works at Baba's slaughterhouse.

HASEENA
Sweet sixteen. Studying hard for medical school. Lives in the building opposite "Baba's Chicken Centre."

VANCOUVER

ABDUL
Hasan's brother. In his thirties. Works (illegally) as a cook in a Mughlai restaurant in Vancouver.

DOC
A surgeon originally from Bombay; fifties. Batsman.

RAM
Thirties. Young, successful banker. Batsman and Bowler.

RANDY
South Indian male, forties. Captain. Team sponsor. Batsman.
Wicket Keeper.

SAM
Thirties. Chinese. Has very little talent, but the team allows
him to play anyway.

The action of the play takes place between a chicken centre in
Bombay and the locker room of the West Coast Cricket Club
in Vancouver.

The year is 2014.

The Men in White makes its debut at the Arts Club Theatre Company's Granville Island Stage in Vancouver, B.C. Hasan (Nadeem Phillip) is not impressed as Baba (Sanjay Talwar) waxes philosophical.

Hasan describes his aspirations for a new life in Vanouver to the brilliant Haseena (Risha Nanda).

Sam (Raugi Yu), Tony (Kamyar Pazandeh), Abdul (Shekhar Paleja), Doc (Munish Sharma), Randy (Parm Soor), and Ram (Anousha Alamian) enjoying a drink after a hard-fought game.

ACT ONE

1.

Mumbai. Dongri. A tough, predominantly Muslim neighbourhood.

Busy, busy, busy. Lots of street hawkers selling everything from cell phones to cutlery.

The focus of the action is Baba's Chicken Centre. A large cage with live chickens in it, packed shoulder to shoulder. The top of the cage is at waist level for HASAN. *He is eighteen years old. He wears an apron covered in blood. Flies are buzzing around his face. The chickens in the cage are surprisingly calm considering that the slaughter is taking place just above their heads.*

BABA, *in his sixties, the owner of the slaughterhouse, is standing next to Hasan, reading an Urdu newspaper.*

It is a hot, stuffy summer afternoon in the last week of May, 2014.

HASAN   There's too many of them. Too many of them.

But Baba's not interested. The paper is keeping him engrossed.

We need to do something.

BABA   Hah? Too many of what?

HASAN   Flies.

BABA   *Not interested,* Okay.

HASAN   We need a fan here.

BABA   A fan? Why do you need a fan?

HASAN   For the flies.

BABA   The flies are feeling hot?

HASAN   They keep sticking to my face.

BABA   So what? That's part of the job.

HASAN   My job is to make a clean cut. That's my job.

BABA   And my job is to tell you to shut up. You young
              people complain too much.

HASAN   *To himself,* Here we go again.

BABA   What did you say? Try not to be cheeky.

HASAN   I'm not being cheeky. These flies are. They sit on
              my cheek all day. As though they are kissing me.

BABA	Why is everything about kissing with you people? In our days, we did not speak like that. We just did our work, we ate, and we died. *Beat.* That shut you up, didn't it?
HASAN	Baba, I need to talk to you.
BABA	Isn't that what we are doing right now?
HASAN	I need you to pay attention.
BABA	Fine. What is it? The way you bully me, I wonder who the boss is.
HASAN	You are the boss, Baba. You are the boss, no doubt. The king. The Badshah of all chickens.
BABA	What do you want, lunatic?
HASAN	Why do you think I want something?
BABA	A second ago you were whining about flies and now you are calling me an emperor.
HASAN	A Badshah is not an emperor. He is a bit smaller. And I wasn't whining. I have a complaint.
BABA	Same thing. Badshah and emperor are both kings. Whining and complaints are both the domain of girls. You are a girl, Hasan. Here you

	are, holding that monster knife in your hand, and you are scared of a few flies.
HASAN	It's impossible to have a conversation with you.
BABA	That's what my wife says too. "Talking to you is like talking to a tree. There is just no response." "But at least a tree gives shade," I tell her. "A tree gives fruit, doesn't it?"
HASAN	So, what does she say?
BABA	"A tree can be cut down."
	Hasan smiles.
	Oh, today must be a special day. The sourpuss of Bombay is smiling. The eternal whiner has seen the light!
HASAN	I do smile . . .
BABA	Now, now, don't sulk. What was it you wanted to ask? Hurry up, it's lunch time.
HASAN	You see . . . the thing is . . . my friend Aftab works at this call centre . . . and each year they do his interview. They ask him questions like, "Are you happy here?" "What challenges do you face on the job?" "Is there anything we can do to make things better for you?"

BABA   Who asks him this?

HASAN   The owner of the call centre.

BABA   Why? Are they bored?

HASAN   No, it is called . . . it is called something. I
            forgot.

BABA   It's called a hallucination. It happens in the
            desert.

HASAN   Appraisal! That's what it's called.

BABA   So what does this have to do with you? Or me?

HASAN   I want you to do my appraisal.

BABA   This is not a call centre.

HASAN   It's a chicken centre. "Baba's Chicken Centre."
            Right?

BABA   *Cocking his ear,* Can you hear that?

HASAN   What?

BABA   What the chickens are saying. Even they are
            saying you are talking shit! They are saying you
            are so boring that they'd rather have their
            throats slit right now than listen to you.

HASAN   But you must do my appraisal. I deserve it. I am your best employee.

BABA   You are my *only* employee!

HASAN   Which makes me the best!

BABA   Fine. Fine. You're giving me a headache. So, are you happy here?

HASAN   What?

BABA   The interview has started, moron. Are you happy here?

HASAN   Well, I . . .

BABA   Yes or no?

HASAN   Yes, I am grateful that you have looked after me and —

BABA   Grateful is not happy. Are you happy or not?

HASAN   No. No, I'm not.

BABA   Is there something I can do to make you happier?

HASAN   Yes, Baba. I need a raise. Based on my performance, I feel —

BABA	What performance? You're not a singer. You cut the throats of helpless animals. What performance is there?
HASAN	But I need a raise.
BABA	Will that make you happy?
HASAN	Yes. Yes, of course.
BABA	Okay then.
HASAN	Okay? You will give a raise?
BABA	Of course not. But at least I did your appraisal.
HASAN	But I need more money!
BABA	What for? You hardly have friends, so you don't go out. You don't have a woman. You get free food from me. What do you need more money for?
HASAN	I want to buy a bat.
BABA	Again you have started this bat business?
HASAN	In the last game, I hit the ball out of the ground. When I connect, the ball just goes into space!
BABA	That's great, that's great. Hopefully, that same

ball will land on your head and knock some
sense into you.

HASAN   When I was little, you told me to dream. You
         said I could do anything I wanted.

BABA   That did not include cricket.

HASAN   What's wrong with cricket?

BABA   Look around you. Tell me what you see.

HASAN   What do you mean?

BABA   Just do as I ask. Describe what you see.

HASAN   I see . . . I see Yakub over there selling pens. His
         brother is selling refills. His brother-in-law is
         selling toys. I see that Pathan is collecting a loan
         from a shopkeeper. I see —

BABA   Are any of these people destined for greatness?

HASAN   How should I know?

BABA   Do they look like they have been on the cover of
         a magazine? Are Yakub's ball pens world
         famous?

HASAN   No.

BABA	Will they ever be?
HASAN	*Disappointed,* No. But *bhai jaan*'s in Canada. He's playing cricket, isn't he? *To himself,* At least he managed to get out of here.
BABA	So now you want to get out of here?
HASAN	I just want to see my brother. It's been years.
BABA	Look, I miss him too. But he has his own journey. And you have yours.
HASAN	*This* is my journey? To be stuck here, with you?
BABA	Hasan, tell me something. What's your name?
HASAN	What?
BABA	Your name. Your full name.
HASAN	You know my full name.
BABA	Just say it out loud for me.
HASAN	Hasan Abdullah Siddiqui.
BABA	Hasan Abdullah Siddiqui. Now, with a name like that, do you think they will allow you into the country? The minute they hear that name, even if you don't have a beard, they'll paint one

on you. Nice and long, like Santa Claus. So, Mr.
Hasan Abdullah Siddiqui, with your name, you
stay here. With me, in Dongri. You are safe
amongst your own. This is not the time to go
frolicking about in Western lands. If you both-
ered to read the papers, you'd know.

HASAN   You're mean.

BABA   I mean well.

HASAN   But I just want —

BABA   Yes, yes, you want. You want a fan, you want a
            bat, you want to play cricket, you want to go
            meet *bhai jaan*. You want, you want, you want.
            You belong to a generation of wanters. You
            want, but you don't know what you *need*.

HASAN   And *you* do?

BABA   Yes! You need a girl! To make you think
            straight! Normally, it's the opposite. Normally,
            women make you lose your mind completely,
            but in your case that's what you need. You see?

HASAN   You know what I see? I see an old man who
            does not want me to succeed.

BABA   And I see Haseena coming this way.

HASAN	What? No.
BABA	Yes, there she is, the girl of your dreams, coming to buy a chicken.
HASAN	Shit. Shit. Shit.

Hasan adjusts his apron.

How do I look?

BABA	Like someone who kills chickens for a living.

Hasan runs his fingers through his hair.

Perfect. Now you have blood on your forehead. Women love that.

HASAN	I hate you.
BABA	Don't worry, today I will help you out. It's time to take this love story forward.
HASAN	Look, if you say a word, a single word, I'll —
BABA	You'll what? Bring it up at your next *appraisal*?

Baba cracks up at his own joke.

HASAN	Look, I'm sorry. I won't ever . . . just don't —

BABA   Relax, I was joking. She's not coming.

              Hasan heaves a sigh of relief.

HASAN   I'm not ready for her today.

BABA   Relax, relax.

              But Baba is lying.

              HASEENA *enters.*

HASEENA   Greetings, Baba. How are you?

              *Upon seeing her, Hasan turns his back and starts
              doing something completely irrelevant.*

BABA   Greetings, my child. How are you?

HASEENA   Busy. I'm studying.

BABA   Studying? But aren't your exams over?

HASEENA   Yes. My tenth-year finals. But I'm so nervous
              waiting for the results that I've already started
              studying for college.

BABA   Good, good. By any chance, are you studying
              mathematics?

HASEENA   Yes, I am. Why, Baba?

BABA   Oh, in case you need help with it.

HASEENA   I did not know you were good at mathematics.

BABA   Me? No, not me. What do I know? I was talking
                about my genius assistant here. He is very good
                at counting chickens.

                *Hasan is furiously cleaning his apron, his back
                still turned to Haseena.*

                Hasan, we have a customer. Please turn around.

                He finally does, slowly, agonizingly.

                Please greet the young lady. Show some respect.

HASAN   Greetings, my child.

                Hasan is horrified that he has blown it.

                They are now both achingly silent. Shy.

BABA   You know, when I first met my wife, there was
                a similar awkwardness.

HASAN   *Glaring,* Baba . . .

BABA   Which reminds me, it's time for lunch. Can't
                keep the old crocodile waiting. You know, I
                never understood the difference between a

crocodile and an alligator until I met my wife. Do you know what the difference is? Crocodiles are more aggressive. *To Haseena,* I say this with love, Haseena. After forty years together, I love my crocodile more than ever. Hasan and Haseena . . . the names just fit.

HASAN   *To Haseena,* Can I please help you with a chicken?

BABA   *To Hasan,* Is that a hint for me to be silent? *To Haseena,* Do you know what his name is? The one I have given him?

Haseena is clearly enjoying Baba's company. She shakes her head.

The Eternal Whiner. *To Hasan,* I was reading today about this girl who stood up to the Taliban. She got an award for it. A Nobel Prize.

He holds up the newspaper.

You should read about her. Her name is Malala. She stood up to the Taliban. A girl. Telling the Taliban to go to hell. Did she complain about a few flies in her face? She had a gun in her face, you moron. Now help the young lady with a chicken.

He exits, leaving the two together.

HASAN   I'm sorry, I . . .

HASEENA   It's okay.

HASAN   He's very old. So, you have come to buy a
            chicken?

HASEENA   Yes . . .

HASAN   We have chickens. As you can see, we have so
            many, very many chickens. *Beat.* I'm sorry, I'm
            not myself today. I . . . it's okay . . . what?

            But Haseena hasn't said a word.

            I thought you said something.

            *Hasan is now resigned to the fact that he has
            completely blown his chance with her.*

            Never mind. Just point.

HASEENA   To what?

HASAN   Which chicken you want. I will prepare it for
            you.

            She points. He gives her a token.

            Number twenty-seven. Come back in sometime,
            I will have it ready.

HASEENA	I'll stay.
HASAN	Okay. Thank you.

He starts cleaning his knife.

	I just wanted a fan, that's all.
HASEENA	What?
HASAN	I don't whine. I just wanted a fan. To keep the flies away.
HASEENA	A fan?
HASAN	Yes, a fan. I don't want you to think I'm a complainer. I don't complain. Only girls complain, you know.
HASEENA	Only girls complain. I see.
HASAN	No, no, I did not mean it . . . I did not mean *you*. I meant girls in general.
HASEENA	I think I'll come back.
HASAN	Yes . . . yes, that would be best. Thank you. Have a good morning.
HASEENA	It's afternoon.

HASAN   Yes, yes . . . of course . . . how right you are . . .

She leaves.

"I just wanted a fan?"

To chicken, Why don't *you* kill *me* instead? Right now, you have more reason to live.

2.

Vancouver, British Columbia, Canada. The last week of May 2014.

The changing room of the West Coast Cricket Club. A large, grimy room with benches, a bathroom, shower stalls, a sink, and an open garbage bin.

SAM enters. Thirty, Chinese, dressed in tracks, a vest, and slippers. He has a healthy paunch but still wears the vest proudly.

He drags a large bag, which contains his cricket kit. He looks at the empty room. Then at his watch.

SAM   *To himself,* Why am I always early? Even when I'm late, why am I early?

RAM   *From offstage,* Because you're too eager.

           Enter RAM. *Sam is pleased to see Ram. Ram is*
           about the same age as Sam.

           You're just too eager, man.

SAM   Fuck you.

           They hug.

           Where is everyone?

RAM   It's just you and me, bro. After last year's
           drubbing, no one wants to play anymore.

SAM   I'll play with you anytime.

RAM   Why did I not like the sound of that?

DOC   Hello, boys!

           Enter DOC. *A powerful presence. Fifties.*

SAM   Hi, Doc!

           Sam turns to hug Doc. Doc just offers his hand to
           Sam.

DOC   A simple handshake will suffice.

RAM	*To Sam,* It means "Will do."
SAM	What?
RAM	"Suffice." That's what it means.
SAM	I know what it means. I'm not dumb. *To Doc,* So, Doc, how was India?
DOC	Good, good, you know, everyone's excited. The feeling is that the PM's going to clean things up. There's hope in the air. Apart from the smog and pollution, there's hope.
SAM	Great. How's the chick scene there?
DOC	I don't know, Sam. I didn't go there for the chicks. I went there to attend my nephew's Navjote ceremony.
SAM	His what?
DOC	It's like a bar mitzvah for my people. An initiation into the Zoroastrian faith.
RAM	Hey, I've attended one of those. Lots of drinking, very little faith.
DOC	What can I say? We like to celebrate.
RAM	Hey, wasn't Freddie Mercury Zoroastrian?

DOC   I'd say he's the world's most well-known
            Zoroastrian. Along with Zubin Mehta.

SAM   Who?

DOC   He's a conductor.

RAM   *To Sam,* Of an orchestra.

SAM   I'm not into classical music.

DOC   And I'm not surprised.

            *Enter RANDY. A South Indian in his forties. He is
            accompanied by ABDUL. Thirties.*

RAM   *Indicating Randy,* Guys, the money has arrived!
            Mr. Randy Prasad! Maker of the best *idlis* in
            Canada!

RANDY   And *dosas.* Don't forget my *dosas.*

            Randy shakes hands with Doc. Sam greets Abdul.

            To Ram, So how come you're on time today?
            Waking up early now?

RAM   Haven't slept, man. At all. Just dropped this
            chick off and now I'm here.

RANDY	You had a date?
RAM	Really nice Russian girl. We just hit it off. It was crazy.
RANDY	You met a really nice Russian girl?
RAM	Yup. She had that great Ukrainian feel to her.
RANDY	They're two different countries. And I don't think they get along.
RAM	She could be Czechoslovakian then. I didn't ask, man.
RANDY	You went on a date and you don't know where she's from?
RAM	Why bring ethnicity into it? We're all human. We're all —
RANDY	Was she a hooker by any chance?
RAM	No. *Beat. Yes!*
RANDY	Why can't you ever get laid without paying?
RAM	Look at me!
RANDY	You have a point.

DOC   *To Ram,* I love your honesty. To openly say that
          you are unwanted — totally and utterly undesir-
          able — is an act of courage.

RAM   I said it in jest. I wasn't . . . *Reminiscing,* She was
          really sweet. We licked wine all night.

DOC   Sipped.

RAM   No, we licked it. Off each other. Best way to
          make cheap wine taste better.

RANDY   *Indicating Sam,* Any way you can make this guy
          play better?

SAM   Hey, come on. I did my job as opener last
          season.

RANDY   If by "did your job" you mean you played like a
          turd, then yes.

SAM   I was told to stay out there for as long as
          possible.

RANDY   And make some runs in the process! You stayed
          so long you had fungus around your toes!

SAM   But you told me to take my time! You said runs
          didn't matter. Didn't you? "Sam, as long as you
          stay there, I'm happy." That's what you said.

RAM	Let's just forget last season.
RANDY	Forget? It's hard to forget. I had a dog, and he died last season. I've forgotten him. But I haven't forgotten how badly we lost. *Beat.* But as captain of this team, I take full responsibility. I've decided to make some changes to our batting order. Instead of Abdul opening the batting, we're going to send him lower down the order. He's going to be our finisher.
DOC	But who'll open the batting with Sam? Sam's an opener, sure, but he's not really an opener. *To Sam,* No offence.
SAM	Offence still taken.
DOC	And the one who can bat, we're sending down the order.
RANDY	That's the reason I called this meeting. I have an idea.
DOC	Let's hear it then.
RANDY	The whole team isn't here. I need the support of the entire team for this one.
DOC	Where the hell are they?

Randy checks his phone.

RANDY	A couple are stuck on the Lions Gate Bridge. The rest have hangovers.
DOC	Well, we're here, so . . .
RANDY	Fine. We're going to bring in an overseas player.
DOC	You mean a professional?
RANDY	Not exactly. He isn't professional, but he's very good.
DOC	You know him?
RANDY	No, I don't.
DOC	So you've just seen him play.
RANDY	I haven't, actually.
DOC	You don't know him. You haven't seen him play.
RANDY	But I'm told he's phenomenal.
DOC	By whom?

Abdul steps forward, humbly. Abdul is a simple presence, very aware of the fact that he is different from the rest of the players. His clothes and body language give the impression that he does not have the same status as the others.

24

When Abdul speaks, it's clear his English isn't as fluent as the rest. But there is a simple poetry and rhythm to his speech. Having picked up words and phrases unconsciously, he assembles them in his own way.

ABDUL   By me.

DOC   So you know the guy?

ABDUL   My brother, Hasan.

DOC   I didn't know you had a brother.

ABDUL   Younger brother. He back in Dongri. In Bombay.

DOC   Oh, I know where that is. Not too many cricketers there.

ABDUL   He chicken cutter.

DOC   I'm sorry?

ABDUL   He work chicken cutter. But great player. If you think I bat good, he bat like a . . . like a storm. Solid power.

RANDY   Look, if Abdul says he's good, then he's good.

ABDUL   He not good. He madman in jungle. He make

shot out of nowhere. *Good length ball* he hit for six. He hit fast bowlers like they spinners. Like they bowling lollipops.

RANDY   But we need to work out the logistics. Visas and stuff.

RAM   I have a contact at the Canadian consulate in New Delhi. I'll find out the details.

RANDY   That's great. But we still need a yes from the rest of the team. And the club president has to approve.

RAM   Then let's discuss that at my place. Tonight. Call the whole team! Drinks are on me. And as a bonding exercise, we'll watch *Gladiator.* That final battle should set our balls on fire.

SAM   I *love* Kurt Russell!

          Sam grabs a cricket helmet from his kit and puts it on.

RAM   Russell Crowe!

          Sam, playing Russell Crowe, turns to everyone.

SAM   *Removing his helmet,* My name is Maximus Decimus Meridius. Commander of the armies

of the North, South, East, and West. Father to a
murdered son —

But Randy holds Sam's helmet.

RANDY   You're this close to getting thrown off the team.
Now. Let's start the season off on a positive
note. Bring it in, guys. Bring it in.

*They all form a circle and place their hands in the
centre. Randy hands out a cigarette to each
player. They light up.*

One, two, three . . .

ALL   West Coast!

*They burst out of the circle, watch the smoke
make circles the way children watch smoke at a
campfire.*

Sam smokes through the ribs of his helmet.

RAM   I think we should work on our stamina this
season.

SAM   *Coughing,* Yup.

3.

Baba's Chicken Centre.

A week later.

Hasan is staring at the building opposite. He is holding large knife in his hand, but it is stationary, as though he were about to bring it down but then got paralyzed.

Baba looks at Hasan.

BABA   The chicken is waiting.

HASAN   Hah?

BABA   Bring that knife down, will you? *Beat.* Is there something on your mind?

HASAN   No, I was staring at the moon.

BABA   It's daytime.

HASAN   Sometimes the moon can be seen during the day, can't it?

BABA   Is the moon sixteen years old by any chance? And does she live in that building opposite?

HASAN   It's been a week. I haven't seen her in a week.

BABA	All these years you saw Haseena but never spoke to her. Why the sudden interest? If I remember correctly, you once said to me that she's "irritating."
HASAN	She was. Once she just took our cricket ball and ran away. Highly irritating.
BABA	You don't seem "highly irritated" now.
HASAN	I don't know, okay? Suddenly all her pimples have gone and now she's . . . I mean they're still there, a couple of them, here and there, but I *like* them. I like her pimples, even. There's something wrong with me.
BABA	Her pimples have burst, and soon your bubble will too. She's out of your league. She speaks English. Fluently.
HASAN	To me she speaks Hindi, no? The language of love. So what's the problem?
BABA	*Money* is the language of love, you idiot. And in that you are even less fluent.
HASAN	She's not even come to the window. Doesn't she need oxygen? *Beat.* Why did you have to behave that way?
BABA	What way?

HASAN   You made me look like a fool.

BABA   No one can make you look like a fool. You have
         a natural talent for being idiotic.

HASAN   There you go again. You're always putting me
         down.

BABA   Just relax.

HASAN   How can I relax when she's stopped buying
         chickens?

BABA   Maybe she is reeling from your beauty. Maybe
         the sweet scent of Hasan has entered her
         nostrils and made her swoon.

HASAN   The scent of Hasan? Do you know what Hasan
         smells like?

BABA   A rose petal?

HASAN   Hasan smells of dead poultry. Each chicken,
         before it dies, farts in my face as a final
         gesture.

BABA   Don't let them get to you.

HASAN   I'm killing them, Baba. A little fart is justified.

BABA   Listen, chickens are not meant to grow old. Give

them a swift, loving death. That's what the chickens told me.

HASAN   The chickens told you this.

BABA   Through the eyes, Hasan. Through the eyes. Everything can be said through the eyes. Your mistake — you did not look Haseena in the eye.

HASAN   She's not a chicken, Baba.

BABA   My wife is a crocodile. But the love is in the eyes. The eyes cannot lie. When I look into those big beady eyes of hers, I don't need to say anything. The fact that she doesn't let me speak is irrelevant.

HASAN   Is that why you talk so much at the shop?

BABA   You are one to talk. The mention of the word "Haseena" makes you shiver like an epileptic. *Beat.* Haseena.

Baba lets out a tiny shiver.

Haseena.

Baba shivers again.

Baba is about to launch into one more "Haseena," when he sees her approaching.

Haseena!

But Hasan thinks Baba is still mocking him.

HASAN   I will never be like you. I am not scared of any
         woman. Let Haseena come in front of me, I will
         show her. The first time I was nervous because
         you made me that way. Next time she comes I
         will charm her. I will sweep her off her feet.
         Even if all women are crocodiles, I will convert
         them into nightingales. And they will sing my
         praises.

HASEENA All women are what?

Hasan freezes.

HASAN   Oh. No.

HASEENA Crocodiles?

HASAN   Oh, no.

BABA   *To Hasan,* May Allah be with you.

HASAN   Why is this happening to me?

BABA   Hello, my child. It's good to see you. Now if
         you'll excuse me, Hasan will tend to you.

HASEENA I'd rather he not.

| BABA | Now, now, don't be that way. One must always be nice to nincompoops. Allah showers blessings on those who do charity. |

Baba deftly exits. Hasan turns around.

| HASAN | I'm so sorry. You were not meant to hear that. |

| HASEENA | Which part? The one where you call women crocodiles or the one where you sweep me off my feet? |

| HASAN | It wasn't me. *Baba* called his wife a crocodile! |

| HASEENA | Baba's a sweet, kind man. He respects women. |

| HASAN | No, no, he's not sweet and kind. He's — |

| HASEENA | Didn't he bring you up? Didn't he look after you and your brother when you had no one? |

| HASAN | Yes, but — |

| HASEENA | But what? |

| HASAN | I . . . never mind. Just point. |

| HASEENA | *Pointing to a chicken,* I'll take that one. |

| HASAN | *Totally resigned,* I'll keep it ready. |

HASEENA   And while you're at it, ask Allah to teach you
           some respect. Oh, my. I wonder how that hap-
           pened.

HASAN   What?

HASEENA   When I opened my mouth, it was *not* to sing
           your praises.

           She leaves.

HASAN   Shit. Shit. Shit. Bloody shit. Bloody hell. Bloody
           hell of a shit I am in. It's okay, Hasan. Take a
           deep breath. Just think she is a fast bowler. Yes,
           that's it. Think she is a fast bowler and she is
           angry and she has bowled you a bouncer. What
           do you do? You simply duck out of the way.
           That's all. You wait for her to get tired.

           *Haseena is back. But, of course, Hasan cannot see
           that she is.*

           Yes, let her get tired. When she gets tired, *that's*
           when you hit her. Hit her hard.

HASEENA   Now you want to hit me? I just came back to tell
           you that my father said to cut it into smaller
           pieces. Animal!

           She leaves in a bigger huff.

HASAN   That old man is destroying my life.

4.

The locker room. A week later.

From now on, everyone is dressed in whites.

Sam and Abdul are in the room.

Sam is in full cricket gear, ready for the game. He is pacing about with his bat in hand. The game hasn't started yet.

Abdul is seated on the bench. He is watching Sam.

ABDUL   Why you nervous?

SAM   It's the first game of the season. I hate first games.

ABDUL   You should not hate any game. Love all game. First game, last game, all same. All chance to play.

SAM   That's easy for you to say. You always score runs. And you're not even opening with me this time. That makes it worse.

ABDUL   Sam, why you play cricket?

SAM	What do you mean?
ABDUL	You Chinese. Why cricket? Chinese no cricketers.
SAM	As a kid, I was never good at sports. So I didn't have any friends. Except Ram. He moved from India and I moved from China at the same time. He's been my friend since the fifth grade. He let me play cricket with him. It made me feel . . . a part of something. And I saw just how much he loved the game. So it made me want to play even more.
ABDUL	Exactly. You saw him love. You saw him love game. What you doing, this not love. This fear.
SAM	But I am scared, do you mind?
ABDUL	What you scared of? Scoring duck?
SAM	Let's not talk about ducks. I refuse to get out on zero in the first game.
ABDUL	But you will. Because you playing for wrong reason. You don't play because you scared of scoring zero. You play because want to make hundred.
SAM	I've never made a hundred. I never will.

A small pause. Abdul wants to say something, but he is not sure. Then he goes for it.

ABDUL   You know Dongri, right? Dongri area?

SAM   Ram used to talk about it sometimes. I know what it's famous for.

ABDUL   For what?

SAM   Dawood Ibrahim.

ABDUL   Correct. Dawood Bhai. Dawood Bhai in Pakistan now. He stop coming India after bomb blasts in ninety-three. Did you know Bhai policeman's son? Son of honest policeman? But Bhai become underworld don. Whole Dongri proud of Bhai. I hear stories of Bhai from older boys, and I proud too. One day Baba ask me, "What you proud of?" I say, "Baba, he become big man from small place like Dongri." Baba say, "Yes, Bhai become big man from small place. But you don't need to become big man. You need to become *good* man." When I little, Baba tell me parents die in bike accident. But now Baba tell hard truth. My father, he stunt-man. One day, man from Dawood gang come to him. D-Company say we need you ride motor-cycle. D-Company man sit behind you, you ride fast, D-Company kill, you ride faster. Father say no. For seven day, D-Company man come.

Final warning. My father no killer. My father
say no. One night D-Company man kill father.
Mother also bullet. By mistake but. She next to
father. I play cricket to forget. The longer I out
there on pitch, less I think of Baba. Of Hasan.
Of father, mother. So if I get out zero, I feel dou-
ble worse than you. Then all week when I cook,
I piss off. And then food taste pissy. *Beat.* You
want to forget something? You score runs. Runs
help forget.

SAM   No, man. I mean . . . sure, I have things . . . but
      nothing like yours.

ABDUL   Nothing you want forget?

SAM   I can't think of anything.

ABDUL   Thanks Allah for blessed life then. Good luck.

SAM   That's it? How does that help me?

ABDUL   Okay, okay, I give you secret.

SAM   Anything, man. Anything.

ABDUL   People make fun of you. They think you
        stupid . . . right?

SAM   Well . . . I mean . . . sometimes, but —

ABDUL   They think you stupid. *I* think you stupid.

SAM   Oh. Okay then. That's your secret?

ABDUL   Doc keep saying you not opening batsman.
             Randy feel bad for you so he take you in team.
             Treat you like disabled child case. You and Ram
             watch porno on phone all day. You no get chicks
             on own. You loser. Correct?

SAM   I'm beginning to get pissed off with you. And
             just so you know, *everyone* watches porn on
             their phones now. It's like checking the time. It
             just pops up, you know. You're trying to send a
             text to someone and suddenly you have these
             pink nipples in front of you, and your whole day
             goes for a toss and . . . why the hell am I
             explaining this to you? I'm pissed off with you.

ABDUL   Good, good. Now keep all piss, keep all it in
             your stomach, in heart, keep all piss off. On
             cricket field, all bowler your enemy. All bowler
             make fun of you. For watching porn, for spend
             Saturday night alone alone alone, for not good
             at anything, for never winning lottery.

SAM   The lottery?

ABDUL   You win lottery?

SAM   No. Never.

ABDUL	Then bowler fault.
SAM	Okay . . .
ABDUL	Use anger. Use insult. You walk out, you look bowler and you insult! Don't matter who. India, Pakistan, Australia —
SAM	What about China?
ABDUL	China no play cricket. You problem China?
SAM	I'm in love with a Chinese girl. But her father won't let her see me.
ABDUL	Then China just announce entry into world cricket. Her father bowling at you. Her small China father coming for you. He want you dead. He want you choke on noodle. He want you have no tongue to kiss pretty daughter.
SAM	Actually, her father's a really nice guy. I think *she* doesn't like me.
ABDUL	Sam! Attention!
SAM	Sorry.
ABDUL	Forget China. Keep piss off anger.

Abdul takes the bat from Sam.

So, you walk down pitch with bat. You look bowler in eye. "I kill you. I burn your home. I kill your wife. I kill your child. I kill your child's child."

SAM   That's a lot of killing.

ABDUL   But you don't say! You just feel. You look in eyes and feel.

SAM   *Charged up,* Yes, I will burn your house. I will burn your brother. Your father. Your uncle. But I will save you and your wife. Then I will tie you up and make you watch while your wife and I . . . while your wife and I . . . watch porn together on my phone!

          He slams his bat against his pads and strides out in a rage. He is Sam the Batting Machine.

          As Sam exits, Randy enters.

RANDY   What happened to him?

ABDUL   He just excited.

RANDY   That's good. I hate starting on a losing note.

          Doc enters.

DOC   Sam's really pumped up. I hope he lasts out there.

ABDUL   Don't worry, he be out there long time.

RANDY   So, Abdul. I discussed Hasan's situation with
         the boys again. There's two ways of getting him
         into the country. The first option is a bit compli-
         cated. The club has to bring him in an official
         capacity. So, we write a letter saying we are
         importing Hasan Siddiqui to play for us for one
         season.

ABDUL   Oh, he be happy. If letter from club, dream
         come true. How you say here . . . "Awesome!"

RANDY   But for that we have to prove that a Canadian
         cannot do what he does.

ABDUL   But Canadian cannot. Canadian good with ice.
         Canadian, how you say here . . . suck balls in
         cricket.

RANDY   But it's not like Hasan has a professional career
         in India. I mean, he's not playing for any club.
         So there's no proof of experience. And we'd
         have to advertise for one month, locally, in
         three different places, to target the Canadian
         market. It's a pain in the ass. *Beat.* But there's
         a second way.

ABDUL   How?

RANDY   We bring him on a tourist visa. You write a

letter saying that your brother would like to
visit you for a couple of months. And then
he plays.

ABDUL   He no visit me. I illegal here, man! Five years I
hiding in back of restaurant. I report, *I* deport.
I no write letter. I no even have *brother*.

RANDY   What do you mean?

ABDUL   Before coming Canada, I write in form. Zero
family.

RANDY   Why'd you do that?

ABDUL   My sponsor say to do, so I do. *Beat*. Doc, you
write letter for me? Please?

DOC   Well, it's not that simple.

ABDUL   Why? Simple. He come, he play, he go.

DOC   Right.

ABDUL   What you mean, Doc?

DOC   What do I mean about what?

ABDUL   "Right." What that mean?

DOC   For one, from what I've been told, your brother

doesn't even have a bank account. The government wants to see that he has sufficient funds in his account.

ABDUL   I get funds. I do for Hasan.

DOC   How?

ABDUL   My problem. I figure.

DOC   Okay then.

ABDUL   So you give letter? You citizen. You doctor. Respected man. You give letter, Hasan get visa.

DOC   *Crudely imitating Abdul,* No, I no give letter.

RANDY   Hey . . . Easy, Doc.

ABDUL   No, no, let him say what he feel. What you feel, Doc? Tell.

             Doc doesn't respond. Abdul is hurt but realizes he is in no position to start a confrontation. But his hurt and shame don't subside.

ABDUL   *To himself,* Why can't people just speak truth?

             Now Doc latches on.

DOC   You want the truth? I'll give you the truth. I

don't think your brother will go back, okay? I think he'll stay on, just like you. It's people like you who give Indians a bad name. You sneak into this country, you stay on, and you make it hard for people like us.

ABDUL   Like you? Like educated man? Man with money? So I no money, no study, so I thief?

DOC   You said it.

Abdul is upset. His body language is a bit aggressive.

Doc senses this.

What — you want to hit me? That's all your people do. Blood is all you know.

ABDUL   My people?

RANDY   Doc, that's enough.

Doc tries to calm himself. But Abdul continues.

ABDUL   So who my people, Doc? I Indian, you Indian. So who my people? How my people different from yours?

DOC   I'm Canadian.

ABDUL   Say it. You big man. You know names of dis-
        eases. But can't see own disease?

DOC   I'm not blind, Abdul. I can see. I have seen. I've
        seen what you did in Bombay. I saw what your
        people did during the riots!

ABDUL   Say it! Say the name!

RANDY   Guys, this is —

ABDUL   Say it!

DOC   You Muslims! Okay? I will not allow another
        Muslim to enter this country. This is my
        country now. Stay out of it!

        Doc storms out.

RANDY   *To Abdul,* Don't worry about him, man. Ignore
        him. Just focus on the game.

        *Suddenly, Ram enters. He is supporting Sam, who
        is badly hurt.*

        *Sam's face is bleeding. His white shirt is covered in
        blood.*

        Randy immediately gets an ice pack and a towel.

RANDY   What happened?

RAM	He got hit, that's what happened. I have no idea what got into him.
RANDY	What do you mean?
RAM	He played a couple of balls and then just started insulting the bowler. He told him to go watch porn. He said, "Your wife called. She said you forgot your balls at home."
RANDY	What the fuck?
RAM	The next ball the bowler gave him a bouncer straight on the nose.
RANDY	*To Sam,* What the hell is wrong with you?
SAM	*Sounding nasal and in pain,* Ask him!
RANDY	Who?
SAM	Abdul! I was so charged up I forgot to wear my helmet!
RANDY	How much did you score?
SAM	A duck. Zero, man! Zero! A duck *and* a broken nose!

Abdul picks up his bat and his cricket kit.

ABDUL   I win this game for you. I win this game. Abdul
            need to stay there long. Abdul need to forget.

            He leaves.

5.

            Baba's Chicken Centre. A day later.

            *Hasan is cutting chickens. He looks totally
            depressed.*

            Baba is reading the newspaper.

BABA   Oh. Oh, no.

            He looks at Hasan. Hasan doesn't care.

            Oh. Oh, my.

            *He looks at Hasan again. Hasan does not fall
            for it.*

            Oh dear. Oh God. This is interesting. *Reading
            from paper,* "Local Dongri Boy Embarrasses
            Himself in Front of Girl He Loves. Again." It is
            headline news.

            *Hasan is trying hard not to react. But, of course,
            Baba knows exactly which buttons to press.*

"Hasan Siddiqui, aged eighteen, a total nincompoop, fails to score yet again. In what has to be the most idiotic way to woo a girl, by insulting her, Siddiqui, stunned by his own stupidity, has gone silent. He has stopped talking to his Baba as well, for no reason, even though his Baba was just trying to help. But his Baba, being kind, being benevolent, being compassionate, being just a really, really nice guy, has found a way to give Hasan one last chance at getting love right."

Baba quickly peers over his shoulder, then back at the newspaper. He has caught Hasan's attention a bit.

Don't worry, *khajoor*. You'll get another chance. You're not *completely* useless.

On hearing this, Hasan removes his apron, and is about to leave.

Too late, boy. Too late. *Discreetly,* I have got her chocolates.

Enter Haseena.

HASEENA   Greetings, Baba.

BABA   Greetings, my child. Thank you for coming to see me. I wanted to give you something.

He removes a box of chocolates from under the counter.

That's for you.

HASEENA   Why are you giving me chocolates?

BABA   I can't give you a chicken, can I?

HASEENA   I mean, what are they for?

BABA   For eating, my dear. This fine gentlemen next to me asked me to get them for you. To make up for his lack of manners. And personality. And charm. And—

HASAN   I think she gets it.

HASEENA   But they're so expensive.

BABA   Not to worry. I just cut the same amount from Hasan's pay this month.

HASAN   What?

BABA   *To Hasan,* But you told me to go get them, didn't you?

HASAN   Yes, yes, of course. I meant you didn't have to tell her that. How does it matter who buys?

Who pays, who does not pay, who wins, who loses, how does it matter?

BABA   That's my boy. *To Haseena,* Won't you forgive this dimwit? He is an orphan. Come on. Do it for an old man. Do it for an old man whose bladder is about to burst. Please excuse me, young lady.

He leaves. Before Haseena has a chance to leave as well, Hasan gets into the act.

HASAN   Listen, I'm sorry. I just . . . I just get nervous around you.

HASEENA   Why?

HASAN   Because I smell.

HASEENA   But that's not your smell.

HASAN   I have blood on me.

HASEENA   It's not your blood.

HASAN   I have flies on my lips.

HASEENA   Much better than the words that come out of them.

Hasan smiles.

Oh, you smiled. I have never seen you smile. You always look so serious. Maybe it's because you are such a tough chicken slaughterer.

HASAN   This is not what I do . . .

HASEENA   This is *all* you do. From morning to evening, you are doing this.

HASAN   I'd like to do something else.

HASEENA   Like what? What about college?

HASAN   No, no college for me.

HASEENA   Why not? You don't like studying?

HASAN   I love studying. I love it. It's just that I can't go to school because Baba needs me.

HASEENA   But you do know how to read and write, don't you?

HASAN   Of course. Of course. I read a lot.

HASEENA   Oh, like what?

HASAN   Books. I read books, I read newspaper articles . . . I like to keep abreast, you know. There's lots going on out there.

HASEENA	Where?
HASAN	Er . . . Tell me your name. Your full name.
HASEENA	Why?
HASAN	Just tell me your full name.
HASEENA	Haseena Abdulrahim.
HASAN	Haseena Abdulrahim. Now, with a name like that do you think they will let you into that country?
HASEENA	What country?

He realizes she isn't following at all. Or perhaps he has realized he is a moron.

HASAN	Enough about me. What are your plans?
HASEENA	*Insha'Allah* I will get good marks in my tenth finals and I will get admission into college.
HASAN	You're leaving?
HASEENA	I'm not leaving. The college is just ten minutes away.
HASAN	Oh. Of course.

HASEENA	But I do want to go to medical school. Eventually.
HASAN	Doctor?
HASEENA	Yes, I like studying. *Pointing to him,* And, clearly, I'm comfortable with the sight of blood, so . . .
HASAN	*Disappointed,* Wow, a doctor. You have big plans. Your plans are huge. *To himself,* I could never . . .
HASEENA	You could never what?
HASAN	I could never be a doctor.
HASEENA	You don't have to. It's not what interests you.
HASAN	Why doctor? Why not something else? Something easier, happier. To be surrounded by sick people all the time . . .
HASEENA	That's exactly why. So I can look after my family. My grandmother has been sick for a month. No one can help her. She's in so much pain all day. What if that happens to my parents? Or my children? I don't want to depend on anyone else. It makes me angry.
HASAN	It makes me angry too.

HASEENA   What do you mean?

HASAN   I have to depend on Baba for everything. Even
           I —

           *Just as Hasan is about to complete his sentence,
           we hear the sound of a motorcycle. The rider is
           revving the engine on purpose. We never see him.*

HASEENA   Oh no.

HASAN   Isn't that Mehndi?

HASEENA   You know him?

HASAN   Everyone knows him. He's famous in Dongri.
           But I don't know him personally, no.

           *Hasan gives Mehndi a half-wave, almost
           apologetic.*

HASEENA   If you don't know him, why are you waving?

HASAN   I love his bike. He's just a year older than I am
           and he has his own motorcycle.

HASEENA   I hate that thing. He keeps wanting to take me
           for a ride.

HASAN   You're lucky . . .

HASEENA   What's lucky about it? He's disgusting. His
           shirt's open till his navel. And his hair. Just look
           at his hair. It's longer than mine.

HASAN   It looks cool, *yaar*.

HASEENA   Then why don't *you* sit behind and wrap your
           arms around him?

HASAN   If he bothers you, just ignore him. He'll go
           away.

           *But Mehndi will not relent. He revs the engine
           and blows his horn. A horn to the tune of a Hindi
           song.*

HASEENA   Do you boys think that this will impress a girl?
           This horrifying tune? *To Mehndi,* Look,
           Mehndi.

           *She signals for him to turn the engine off. Once he
           does, Haseena looks around to see if anyone is
           watching. The street is busy as hell but no one's
           really focusing on them.*

           You're a nice guy. You're good looking. Your hair
           is so silky you could do a shampoo ad. But . . .
           but I already have someone. I have a boyfriend.

HASAN   *To himself,* Shit. What shitty luck I have.

HASEENA	*To Mehndi,* And what's more, he bought me a gift. *To Hasan,* Show him the chocolates.
HASAN	*I'm* your boyfriend?
HASEENA	Hurry up or by God I will slit your throat.

Hasan quickly raises the box of chocolates high in the air. Ridiculously high, out of fear, as though he is holding a time bomb.

To Mehndi, There. These cost a lot. These are Belgian chocolates. Do you know where Belgium is? Or when you were reading the map did your hair come in the way?

Mehndi starts his motorcycle and leaves. An angry exit.

What a sample.

HASAN	You shouldn't have done that.
HASEENA	Done what?
HASAN	Insulted him like that.
HASEENA	Insulted *him?* What about his insulting me? You think it's okay for a man to rev his engine like that? To sit on a machine and go *voom-voom-voom,* that's not an insult? To play "*Ek-Do-Teen*"

on his horn to me. Do you know that in the movie Madhuri plays a woman of the night? So isn't that what he's calling me? That's not an insult?

HASAN   Well, if you put it like that . . .

HASEENA   How else should I put it? *Beat.* I was in such a good mood.

HASAN   Here, have a Belgian chocolate.

HASEENA   These are not Belgian chocolates. They're Cadburys.

HASAN   Okay. Sorry.

HASEENA   No, I'm sorry. That fellow is my cousin.

HASAN   Your cousin?

HASEENA   And he still wants to be with me. That's repulsive.

HASAN   But you can go a little easy on him.

HASEENA   Why are you siding with him?

HASAN   I'm not siding with him. I understand him.

HASEENA   You understand that . . . that *thing*?

HASAN	He's just trying to win you over. When a man tries to win the affection of a woman, all his wires go criss-cross. He does stupid things.
HASEENA	Like call her a crocodile?
HASAN	Yes.
HASEENA	Hasan, are you trying to win me over?
HASAN	*In a panic,* What? No. Oh God, no. Why would I try to win you over? You're like a sister to me.
HASEENA	What?
HASAN	What?
HASEENA	You're strange. You are such a strange boy.

She leaves.

HASAN	*To himself,* Sister? Why is she my sister? Why is she your sister? What is *wrong* with you? Why can't you keep your mouth *shut?* Stay calm, Hasan. You are panicking. People are looking at you. You are talking to yourself, calm down! Eat some chocolates, Hasan. Eat some Belgian chocolates.

He opens the box and starts eating.

6.

The locker room. A week later.

The boys are getting ready for a game.

As soon as Doc enters the locker room, Abdul leaves. There is a real edge. Randy decides to address it.

RANDY   Look, guys. If we want to win out there, we have to be united.

Ram and Sam nod their heads. But Doc is silent.

We have to keep our personal differences aside. Only if we play together can we win. Am I clear?

SAM   I have no issue with Abdul. I'm all for a clean start.

RANDY   I wasn't talking about you, but it's okay.

RAM   Actually, you look better with a broken nose. It's almost as if he got a nose job. Right, Doc?

But Doc is silent. He's just putting his gear on.

RANDY   Are we cool, Doc?

DOC   About what?

RANDY   I just need to know that we're cool.

DOC   We're cool.

RANDY   Abdul is an integral part of this team.

Randy's cell phone rings.

DOC   I said I was fine.

RANDY   You don't look it.

DOC   I don't have to be best friends with the guy, do I? It's okay, I'm good.

Randy answers his phone.

RANDY   Hello? Yeah, Randy here. *Beat.* Where the hell are you guys? No one from your team is here, man. *Beat.* What? Why not? *Beat.* Hey ... take it easy ...

He listens some more.

Fuck you!

He disconnects. He is fuming, rattled.

That was the other team. They're not coming.

RAM   What? Why not?

RANDY	They said it's too long a drive to play with a bunch of losers They said they'd rather lose points than play with us. Bastards.
RAM	Ignore them, man. They're just trying to rile you up. They probably didn't have a full team.
RANDY	They made fun of my food! They said my *medu vadas* were putting my team to sleep. Their captain actually said that. I mean, you can insult my kids, that's fine. Call *them* stupid, because they are. But my food? That's just —
SAM	We should complain to the league.
RANDY	I'm sick and tired of having this loser reputation! None of you guys ever come for practice! Let's use this time to practice.
SAM	But it's raining outside.
RANDY	It always rains *outside*. Ever heard of indoor rain?
RAM	Guys — let's just . . . wait for the rain to stop.
RANDY	Fine, let's wait. That's all we keep doing. Waiting. From one game to the next. Oh, we lost this week. No problem, let's *wait* for next week. So we can lose all over again.

RAM	Relax, man. We're not professionals. Let's have fun out there.
RANDY	Fun? Losing isn't fun! Look, I know we're not playing the World Cup, okay? I know we had only two spectators for the whole of last season, one of whom was homeless, but that's not the point. I just—
RAM	That homeless guy stole my phone, man. I saw him hovering around my bag. I can't prove it, but I know it's him.
SAM	Hey, that wasn't a homeless guy. That was my friend, Gary.
RAM	Your friend stole my phone?
SAM	He would never . . . and anyway, it was an Android. I just don't get people who use Androids.
RAM	And I don't get people whose friends look like they're homeless. He had a hole in his pants, man!
RANDY	Fuck, we have no focus! We can't even talk about cricket, let alone play it.
RAM	Dude, you're our captain! You can't get worked up! You should be calming *us* down!

RANDY   That's what I'm trying to do! So calm the fuck
           down!

           Abdul enters.

ABDUL   Schedule change. Our next game next weekend.
           Now we against number one team in division.

RANDY   Great. That's just great.

RAM   On the subject of winning . . . since we're all
           here together . . . I spoke to my contact at the
           Canadian consulate in India. I've figured out
           the details for Hasan's visa. We need a letter of
           leave from his employer. And he has to show he
           has enough funds in his bank account.

RANDY   How much is enough?

RAM   About forty thousand dollars.

ABDUL   What? Where he get forty thousand?

SAM   We could raise the money. Let's think of
           something.

RAM   Raise the money? He's not Terry Fox!

RANDY   Does he have a bank account?

ABDUL   Yes, but account empty. Zero money.

A pause of disappointment. Then —

RANDY   I'll do it.

RAM   Do what?

RANDY   Put money in his account. From India. My man
               Shetty will handle it. Shetty will print out a
               statement to show that regular deposits were
               being made over the last six months. But you
               have to show that this is Hasan's income.
               What's his occupation?

ABDUL   Chicken cutter.

RANDY   No. He's head chef. In my restaurant in Bombay.
               I'll provide a letter. And he's just been given a
               huge cash award in recognition of his outstand-
               ing work.

ABDUL   But he bad, bad cook.

RANDY   No, he's a great cook.

RAM   But there's still one issue though. He has to
               show that he has a valid reason to go back.

RANDY   That's true. Forty grand isn't enough reason
               to go back. Plus that money can always be
               transferred here. *To Abdul,* So you think of
               something, okay?

ABDUL   Are you sure? That lot of money.

RANDY   Your brother better be good, man. I want to
            win. I want to tear the opposition's panties and
            stuff them in their mouths.

ABDUL   When Hasan bowls, he so fast opposite panties
            tear on their own. I show you photo.

SAM   Of panties?

ABDUL   Of brother.

            *He reaches into his wallet and takes out a photo
            of him and Hasan.*

RANDY   He doesn't look like he can do shit.

ABDUL   This old photo. He twelve.

RANDY   So Ram, why don't you be Hasan's contact? I'll
            provide a letter as his employer. You give a letter
            of invitation. That way, you and I are not
            connected.

RAM   No problem. I'll say I've known Hasan a long
            time. We used to hang out in Bombay all the
            time.

SAM   You did?

RAM   *To Sam,* I pity you. I love you, but I pity you.

DOC   You know, I have a friend who's coming to town
               this week. He used to play at the state level in
               India. We should try him out.

RANDY   Sure, sure. The more the merrier.

DOC   This guy used to be a mean bowler. Really
               quick.

RANDY   Bring him on, Doc. So here's to two mean
               bowlers.

ABDUL   Hasan all-rounder. Hasan bat and bowl.

RAM   Is there anything he can't do?

ABDUL   *Pointing to Sam,* Yes, he can't score duck.

               They laugh.

DOC   This guy, Ramesh, he used to be in medical
               school with me. He's my age but he can do this
               team some good.

RANDY   Sure.

DOC   We both did our internship together in Bombay
               many years ago at JJ Hospital.

ABDUL   Oh . . . JJ very close to my home.

DOC   *Not really responding to Abdul,* JJ's a tough place.
We had guys come in with broken heads.
Young, sixteen, seventeen years old . . . there
was this girl who came in, Hema. She was by far
one of the prettiest women I'd ever seen. When
I saw her face, it was . . . how can I describe
it . . . if you took the moon and polished it, and
then polished it again, and then added a bit of
sun, that's what she looked like. When she came
in, we just froze. We had never seen anything
like her. She was pregnant. But she wasn't deliv-
ering. Not exactly. She just had her belly slit
open, across the waist, from here to here, and
the head was out . . . we could see the head. She
was brought in by her husband who was shiver-
ing, "Please, doctor, do something, please." So
what could we do, except let her die? That was
the only thing we could do. They had slit open
her belly with a sword. This was during the
Hindu-Muslim riots. JJ's in a predominantly
Muslim area, you see, and she was Hindu, so
she had to die. It was the sensible thing to do.

RANDY   That's enough.

ABDUL   So what you saying?

DOC   I'm not saying anything. I'm just telling a story.
About my friend Ramesh and me.

ABDUL I not like this.

DOC Well, I guess I'm not a good storyteller.

ABDUL I think you good storyteller.

DOC Oh, thanks.

ABDUL I think you know how to tell story. In good story, you make up things. You good.

DOC You think I'm making it up? Why would I be making it up?

ABDUL To make me look bad. To make brother look bad.

DOC I don't need to do that. Your own people did that for you.

When he hears this, Abdul goes for Doc.

ABDUL *Bhenchod!*

He tears across the room, but Randy and the guys get to him in time.

DOC Come on, hit me! *Beat.* Oh, I forgot! You won't hit me! I'm not pregnant!

END OF ACT ONE

ACT TWO

1.

A week later.

The locker room.

Everyone is present. Except Doc.

Randy is using a device the size of an iPhone to project a video onto the wall. But it isn't working.

SAM   *To Ram,* Hey, are we watching a movie?

RAM   We should watch *E.T.*

SAM   *Fist pump,* Yeah. *E.T.* . . .

RAM   Hey Randy, have you seen *E.T.*?

RANDY   No.

RAM   You serious? Every immigrant *has* to watch *E.T.*

RANDY   What the hell are you talking about?

RAM   It's a movie about exile, man. The longing to go back home. That little guy wants to go back to his own country, touch his own soil, drink his own chai, talk in his native language . . . I got it when I was a kid, but the other kids just saw him as an alien.

RANDY   He *is* an alien. A mechanical puppet.

RAM   Someone should write a paper on it. If you think about it, in the end, *he* made the white kids fly. This brown wrinkly thing . . .

SAM   *Whispering to Ram but super loud,* Yeah, his skin looked like shrivelled testes, dude.

RANDY   I hope you two die young.

          Randy is done setting up the video.

          There! Done!

          He faces the others.

          What does cricket mean to you?

SAM   To me, it means —

RAM   It's a rhetorical question. He's trying to give a speech.

SAM   How should I know?

RAM   Because no one else answered, bro. It was in the
             tone. Try and understand tone.

RANDY   I'm going to poison you both, okay? Let's try
             this again. What does cricket mean to you?

             *They all look at Sam. This time he does not
             answer.*

             Thank you. I could bore you with a speech, but I
             won't do that.

             *On the wall, we see a crazy mash-up of cricket at
             its wildest, its most aggressive — an array of
             bouncers, catches, run-outs, jaw-crushing inju-
             ries, and massive sixes — set to a blistering
             soundtrack. It's just music, no commentary.*

             This is what cricket is about. You get hit, you get
             up, and *you* start hitting. Watch it again and
             again. Get inspired!

             *While the guys are soaking it in, Abdul steps
             forward.*

ABDUL   While Doc not here, I say something. I sorry
             I get angry last time. I never hit anyone ever.
             Only thing I hit is ball, out there. Only thing
             I hit.

RANDY   It's okay.

ABDUL   No, but you guys team, you guys need know
          why Abdul get angry.

RAM   We trust you, man.

ABDUL   The man I work for . . . he my sponsor for tour-
          ist visa. He from my area in Dongri. Six years
          ago, he come to my Baba and say he take me to
          Canada. He starting Mughlai restaurant, he
          need cook. I chicken cutter, but I also good
          cook. I agree only if he bring my Hasan also . . .
          we both start new life, make new money. My
          owner, he promise me brother come. But first,
          me. All day I live in kitchen. One day while I
          work in restaurant, immigration come. So what
          I do? I sit down in restaurant like customer. I
          pretend but I so scared I eat remaining food
          from someone plate. I so scared I no realize I
          chewing only chicken bones. When two other
          customer leave, I go also, hands of chicken
          bone . . . how I feel? That day, I cry for home, I
          cry but no sound come. My owner he see hand
          shaking, he understand. He take me drive, see
          Vancouver, how beautiful city. He make me sit
          in front seat, and my hand still shaking, still no
          sound, but then . . . I see this water, this blue
          blue water, and then I circle along water, along
          side of road and I see . . . I see men in white, I
          see but I no believe, white on green field, grass
          like soft bed, no stones like in Bombay *maid-
          aan*, and I think, no, these not men, these

angels. In Quran, they say paradise for us, but this paradise, here. I beg stop car and I get out, and I think how possible in Canada? And he say, oh they play every Sunday, and I ask what ground this, and he say Stanley Park, and how Sir Donald Bradman, greatest cricket batsman all time, he come here in thirties, and he say this most beautiful ground he ever play on, Sir Donald say this, and I feel okay if my owner no treat me right, I feel okay if my owner pay less, I get to touch soft, green bed, I feel with my hands, first time I feel like home, I feel welcome here in cold country. Grass smile at me, people no smile me, but grass smiling. So I get back in car and I smile too. What me saying, me not come Canada as thief, my owner he bring, he promise legal, he promise legal. What type life I have, no see Hasan, but now have you guys, so when Doc say about JJ, what have to do with me? But Doc he make me liar . . .

RANDY *To Abdul,* It's no trouble. We're all immigrants here.

ABDUL But I no immigrant. I thief feel like.

RAM Come on . . .

ABDUL All this time, Hasan ask me on phone, "Where you stay? Show me your house. Show me your area." But what I show him? That I live in back of restaurant? That I hide like rat? I no tell him truth. Baba no tell him. But he come here, he *see* truth. After *abba* and *ammi-jaan* gone, I suppose look after Hasan. But — but I no even look after myself! Maybe he need to see . . . One summer. From big brother to Hasan. Please. Personal guarantee. He score, he make you win, he go back. I promise he go back.

The guys see the pain in his face. Randy steps up.

RANDY   Abdul, when my father brought me here, I was a South Indian kid in a country that felt whiter than snow. My folks had cash, but you can't wear that cash on your face, your cash don't change your colour, it don't make you white. Now, I'm not one for this bullshit about white people not accepting me. Why should they accept me? Did they invite me to Canada? Did they say, "Hey, Randy, come on over"? No. If a white dude comes to India, we roll out a carpet for him, but only because we've been colonized and computerised to do it. That's changing now. But fuck that too. The white kids in my school ignored me. They weren't mean to me, they just ignored me. I didn't exist. Now my real name isn't Randy. It's Randi. In Telegu, Randi means "Welcome." But you know what it means in Hindi? "Whore." Of course, the white kids didn't know this. But our *desis* were kind enough to enlighten them. Every single day,

Randi, Randi, Randi. My own people. The ones
who were born here, who have the right accent
but the wrong colour. When I look at Doc I see
that brown kid in school who wants to love
India, but doesn't know how to, and he wants to
love Canada too, but he doesn't know how to. So
I don't give a flying fuck-and-a-half about what
Doc says, or thinks. In my book, your brother is
welcome here. Will he have to go back?
Absolutely. I'll make sure he does. But while he's
here, he's one of us.

RAM   Your parents should have done a better job of
             naming you, bro. I mean do a little research, for
             God's sakes.

RANDY   It's okay. They're dead now.

RAM   Oh. I'm sorry.

RANDY   I'm kidding. They're alive. But it's time they
             went. They're both really old. It's like looking
             into your future. It's like *me* looking at *me* years
             from now. It's painful.

             Everyone is enjoying the shift in mood, except
             Abdul.

ABDUL   Listen . . . I worried about Doc. If he report I be
             in trouble . . .

RANDY   Don't worry, I'll talk to him.

RAM   We all will.

ABDUL   I don't know how say thanks . . . I so grateful . . .

         Sam sees an opening.

SAM   *In Scottish accent,* I am William Wallace! And I
         see a bunch of losers in front of me. You came
         to Canada as free men but you can't live here for
         free, can you? It's bloody expensive. And centu-
         ries from now, sleeping in your hammocks,
         dying, coughing, sneezing, shivering, watching
         that loonie drop, are you willing to surrender it
         all, for just one chance, one chance, to hit that
         ball, to wear white, a colour that gets dirty so
         easily, to play a pointless game that goes on for-
         ever, a game that no one understands — are you
         willing to surrender all that? So go tell our
         enemy that they may take our *wives* but they
         may never take our cricket!

RANDY   *To Abdul,* Just tell your brother he'll be here.

2.

The chicken centre. A day later.

*Hasan is grumbling away as he takes the
butcher's knife and cuts the meat into pieces.*

Baba, as usual, is reading the paper.

HASAN   It's not my fault that I ate the chocolates. I was
        nervous. But no, you can't let it go. You are an
        unforgiving old man.

        Baba turns the page.

        And your chocolates weren't that good anyway.
        They made my stomach grumble.

BABA   I understand why you are this way.

HASAN   What way?

BABA   Why your hormones are raging.

HASAN   Nothing is raging.

BABA   You were supposed to give the chocolates to *her*.
        And you young people call *us* senile. You're lazy
        too. Hurry up with the cutting.

        Hasan gets back to cutting.

Remember, two chickens for Naguib to be delivered by noon at the restaurant. And two for Aslam Bhai, and one for Ghulam Ali, both home deliveries. And make sure you take off your apron when you go. You sometimes forget to take off your apron. It scares the children. Are you listening?

But Hasan doesn't answer.

Boy, are you listening?

Hasan suddenly slams the knife down on the chopping board. Baba is shocked.

HASAN   No, I'm not. I'm not listening, okay? I'm done! I'm done with this . . . with this . . .

BABA   Hasan, what is wrong with you?

HASAN   I will not take my apron off! Either they accept me or they don't! I . . . I have to get a job! Something where I . . . I need an office!

BABA   What the hell are you talking about?

HASAN   How will she respect me? She's a doctor. She's a bloody doctor and I'm such a loser. All I asked for was a bat. I just need a bat so I can hit my way to the top! How will I provide for her?

BABA	Calm down, Hasan . . .
HASAN	I won't calm down! I —

As Baba moves towards Hasan, we hear the sound of a motorcycle. Baba's attention has now shifted to the opposite side of the street.

BABA	Who's that there?

Hasan looks.

HASAN	I don't know.
BABA	That fellow on the motorcycle. You don't know who he is?
HASAN	No.
BABA	Then why is he staring at us?
HASAN	Just ignore him.
BABA	I know that chap. He's up to no good. That's Mehndi. He's part of a gang.
HASAN	He's just an idiot with a knife.
BABA	The way he's looking at us . . .
HASAN	Not us. Me. He's looking at me.

BABA   Hasan, are you in trouble?

HASAN   He's after Haseena. He thinks she's his girlfriend.

BABA   Is she?

HASAN   No, are you crazy? My Haseena will never go —

BABA   *Your* Haseena?

HASAN   I meant —

BABA   I hope you didn't say anything to him.

HASAN   I don't associate with him.

BABA   Listen to me, you moron. Even if you don't
              associate, if *he* decides to associate, you will be
              associating whether you like it or not.

HASAN   But I thought you were all about protecting the
              dignity of a woman. What happened? Changed
              your mind?

BABA   Shut up, Hasan. That boy is a good-for-nothing.

HASAN   So I should let him think that Haseena is his?

BABA   Let him think he is Salman Khan. Let him
              think he is an astronaut. Let him think he has
              found a cure for baldness. What do we care?

HASAN   You make no sense at all.

BABA   Of course I do. It's about *association*. I took
          three unrelated things and made a connection.
          Just as he will take his fist, your jaw, and major
          velocity! In any case, let Haseena decide. In my
          humble opinion, it's no contest.

HASAN   Really? Then why did she tell Mehndi that she
          likes me? That *I* am her boyfriend?

BABA   She said that?

HASAN   Like her lips were loudspeakers.

BABA   Don't you know anything about women?
          Anything?

HASAN   Maybe not. But I know Haseena.

BABA   Do you know how male crocodiles get their
          woman? They charm her by bringing their jaws
          down on the water really hard, like this, and
          then blowing water from their noses. You know
          who that is? That is Mehndi. He raises his
          motorcycle, like the jaw, high, comes down on
          the water, *phat*, and blows his horn. Then there
          is you. Low frequency. A grumbling, muttering
          crocodile underwater. Now which one do you
          think the female crocodile will go for? Hah?

HASAN   The motorcycle crocodile.

BABA   Correct.

HASAN   I'm sorry I exploded back there . . . I have no
               idea what's going on.

BABA   Hasan, with your name, try not use words like
               "exploded" in the future.

HASAN   *Dejected,* Who cares? How does it matter now?

BABA   Relax . . .

               *Baba removes an envelope from his shirt pocket
               and offers it to Hasan.*

               Use this to breeze your delicate chin. Then
               perhaps gentler words will emerge.

HASAN   But why can't you just give me a fan instead of
               an envelope?

BABA   Just use it. Trust me.

HASAN   But it makes no sense.

BABA   Perhaps if you opened it . . .

HASAN   I'd rather not. I'd rather have a small fan.

BABA	Listen, you bloody fool, it's a surprise!
HASAN	What surprise?
BABA	Jackass from the stupidest corner of this earth, how will you know if you don't open it? *To himself,* It's okay, relax. This is the nature of youth these days . . .

Hasan opens the envelope.

HASAN	What's this?
BABA	Your bank account.
HASAN	Twenty lakhs? Twenty lakhs? Where did you get so much?
BABA	I sold an extra chicken or two. *Beat.* Oh, never mind. You're going to Canada.
HASAN	To meet *bhai jaan*?
BABA	To play cricket. But you can meet your brother too if you want.
HASAN	*Overwhelmed,* Baba . . .
BABA	Hold on. You still need a visa. Luckily for you, no interview required. They won't see your face. So, better chance.

HASAN   I'm going to Canada!

BABA   Yes.

HASAN   I'm going to Canada!

BABA   Where is Canada? Do you know?

HASAN   Who cares? I'm going!

            *Hasan jumps on Baba, hugging, embracing him
            with all the love he has.*

BABA   It's okay, okay, save the energy for the game.

            *Baba wants to hug Hasan but is feeling awkward
            by this sudden and rare display of physical
            affection.*

            Hasan, people are looking . . . I'm a deadly
            chicken killer . . .

            But Hasan hugs tighter.

            Let go, you fool, you're getting blood on my
            shirt!

            Baba pries himself away.

            Now I will get the scolding of my life!

A beaming Hasan now turns to his chickens.

HASAN   *To chickens,* I'll be meeting *bhai jaan*! I'll be
meeting *bhai jaan*! Wait till I tell Haseena!

He looks to her window and calls her name.

Haseena!

BABA   Hasan, quiet . . .

HASAN   I just want her to know.

BABA   Yes, yes. But not like this. Let her come.

But Hasan is still beside himself.

HASAN   Oh my God! This is incredible. I'll be a foreign
return. I'll be wearing Nike shoes! And I'll have
an accent. I'll say, "Hey . . . " In English. Like
the movies.

BABA   You already have an accent? You haven't even
got a visa yet.

HASAN   I hope I get it!

BABA   You have to show that you have a solid reason
for coming back. But don't worry, I'll think of
something. *Beat.* Hasan, are you sure you want
to go?

HASAN   Of course! Two things I love most: *Bhai jaan*
         and cricket! What's there to think? And you, of
         course, three things I love most. But I already
         have you, so . . .

         He notices that Baba isn't entirely happy.

         What's wrong? Don't you want me to go?

BABA   I don't know, Hasan. With everything that's
         going on in the world right now, maybe you're
         better off here, with me. I can't protect you if
         you go.

HASAN   But *bhai jaan*'s there. He's okay, isn't he? What's
         there to protect?

BABA   He wants to come back!

HASAN   What?

         Baba regrets saying that. He backtracks.

BABA   He misses you. He wants to come back, but he
         can't. He has no choice. What will he come back
         and do? He's trying to save money so that he
         can do something for you . . . I keep telling him
         to let it go.

HASAN   Why are you stopping him from doing some-
         thing for me? Why can't you just let me be?

BABA	When your parents died, I promised myself I would never let anything happen to you. You don't understand!
HASAN	No, I don't! You're always holding me back! You let *bhai jaan* go. You didn't stop him.
BABA	He is much older than you. You were a baby when you . . . I held you as a baby, Hasan.

Hasan can see that Baba is genuinely concerned.

HASAN	Please, Baba. Be happy for me. That's all I ask.
BABA	Hasan, I am not your father. I never will be. I —
HASAN	Don't say that.
BABA	I am just a caretaker. You did not choose me. I chose you. When your parents died, this place was full of gang wars. It was a place where the cost of a life was less than the cost of a knife. Even when Abdul left, I thought he was going to a better place. But things are better here now. I just don't know anymore. When Abdul told me he had made arrangements for you to go there, I got angry.
HASAN	Angry? Why angry?
BABA	Your brother . . . he . . . it's been hard for him.

Sometimes, when I hear his voice on the phone,
it feels like it's coming from so far away . . .

HASAN   He *is* far away.

*Baba goes into a semi-trance. He isn't really
responding to Hasan.*

BABA   That place has done something to him . . . and
I don't know if he will ever get it back . . .

*Hasan seems worried, confused. He has never
heard Baba speak like this.*

HASAN   Get what back?

BABA   He has worked so hard. For what?

HASAN   Baba, what is it that you are not telling me?

BABA   *Lashing out,* I don't know if that place is good
for us! Here, at least you are amongst your own.

*Then, realizing that he is shaking Hasan up, Baba
changes gears.*

Forgive me, Hasan. This is just an old man talking. Never let an old man stop you from living.
Beat. Your mind is made up anyway.

HASAN   Yes, Baba.

BABA	What if I give you a promotion?
HASAN	Baba . . .
HASAN	Make you General Manager?
HASAN	That's too . . . general.
BABA	How about Chief Financial Officer?
HASAN	That sounds much better.
BABA	But you can only *count* the money, not take it. The money stays with me.
HASAN	*Respectfully,* Baba, I have to go. I have to follow my dream. Even if it's for just one season.
BABA	Then at least let me train you for your travels. Otherwise you will not even enter your dream. Now: What word should you not use? Never use?
HASAN	Explode?
BABA	Correct.
HASAN	I'll just say I'm angry.
BABA	No, no, no. They don't like anger. No anger allowed over there. You have to be calm, like

lotus. And no pondering, no thinking too much. It means you're plotting something. And shave every single day! Do you hear me? Not a single hair on your chin.

HASAN   No Santa Claus!

BABA   That's my boy!

Haseena enters. She looks annoyed. Baba exits.

HASEENA   What is wrong with you?

HASAN   Oh wouldn't *you* love to know?

HASEENA   Why are you shouting my name? If my father were home, he'd get really angry.

HASAN   He can't get angry. It's not allowed.

HASEENA   Hah?

HASAN   In Canada. No anger allowed. That's where I'm going.

HASEENA   I know.

HASAN   And I'll be a clean shaven lotus. What — how do you know?

HASEENA   Baba told me.

Hasan is deflated.

HASAN   Why does he . . .

HASEENA   Oh, don't be like that. I've got my computer
          with me. To show you pictures.

HASAN   I don't want to see pictures. I'm going there.
          What will I see pictures for?

HASEENA   So you don't look like a complete villager when
          you land there.

HASAN   And what do you know about Canada?

HASEENA   More than you do. Do you know the name of
          the city your brother is in?

HASAN   Vancouver.

HASEENA   What's the capital of Vancouver?

HASAN   What do I care?

HASEENA   Hasan, how can a city have a capital?

HASAN   No matter what you do today, nothing can
          dampen me. Nothing.

          She opens her laptop.

HASEENA   Here, pictures of Vancouver.

HASAN   Wow, it's green.

HASEENA   Yes.

HASAN   It's really green.

She keeps showing him pictures.

It's really, really . . . *green.* So many trees, so very
many trees.

He points to a corner of the street.

We have *one* tree on this street. And even that,
someone has hung towels on to dry.

HASEENA   Well, don't go there and hang a towel on a tree.

HASAN   No, no, I would be scared too. My towel will
become *green.*

Another picture.

Wow, that's blue.

HASEENA   Yes.

HASAN   That's really blue. Is that real water?

HASEENA	My feeling is, and this is just a feeling, they have added artificial flavor to it.
HASAN	Look at that. A dolphin. You were right. The dolphin is blue. It's like ice candy. You make it whatever colour you want.
HASEENA	Your chickens will become blue if they go to Vancouver.
HASAN	What a place, *yaar*.
HASEENA	This is my favourite. My absolute favourite.

But Hasan doesn't respond.

You don't like flowers?

HASAN	Of course I do. I love flowers.
HASEENA	You love flowers?
HASAN	I mean, no, not as a man. No, of course not. I love them, I *like* them as a thing of beauty. But I don't —
HASEENA	It's okay if you love flowers.
HASAN	Do you want me to love flowers? I'd even eat them if you'd want me to.

HASEENA   These are called tulips.

HASAN   Too lips.

HASEENA   *Tu.*

HASAN   No, too. "Too" means "you" in Hindi. "Lips" is I
            know what. So, it means "Your lips."

            Haseena shyly changes the picture.

HASEENA   This photograph confuses me.

HASAN   What is this?

HASEENA   It's a steam clock.

HASAN   A what?

HASEENA   A clock that gives out steam. It works on steam.
            What I don't understand is why so many people
            are staring at it. See — at least thirty people are
            staring at the steam clock.

HASAN   There must be more to it.

HASEENA   I don't think so. I think this is it. It's just the
            steam.

HASAN   It's quite a mystery.

HASEENA	So what will you do there? Just play cricket?
HASAN	*Just* play cricket? *Just* play cricket? That's all I want!
HASEENA	That's all you want? No. You want a job. A house. A car.
HASAN	You don't understand. The league that my brother plays in, that's the same league in which some of Canada's national players play. If they see me, if they see how good I am, I can play for Canada.
HASEENA	How can you play for Canada? You're Indian.
HASAN	I'll figure it out. Let me just get there.
HASEENA	If you're so good, why not play here? You should be playing here.
HASAN	I tried. You need someone to coach you, you need a school team. I don't go to school. I'm here all day. So, who will take a chance on me? I can't afford a coach. Or a bat or anything. Tendulkar became Tendulkar because he had a great coach. Achrekar Sir was a great coach.
HASEENA	He also had a brother who believed in him. His brother sacrificed his own career so that Tendulkar could become the greatest batsman

of all time. And you *do* have a brother who believes in you.

HASAN   Yes ... true ...

HASEENA   So is Tendulkar your favourite player?

HASAN   Oh, yes, I love Sachin. But he's actually my brother's favourite player.

HASEENA   Who's yours?

HASAN   My favourite player is Tony Greig.

HASEENA   Who?

HASAN   Tony Greig. He was the captain of England in the seventies. Great player. But I like him more for something else. His commentary. No one could speak like Tony Greig. I learnt a lot of English only by listening to him talk about cricket. "Whadda player! Whadda player!"

HASEENA   That's good ... that's good ...

HASAN   "They're dancing in the aisles in Sharjah! The little man has hit the big man for six!"

HASEENA   That's very good, Hasan!

            They both laugh.

But Hasan simmers down.

HASAN   When I was little, I used to imagine that one day Tony Greig will speak about me that way. He will say those words about me with total excitement, as if a part of him is inside me, and when I hit the ball, he hits the ball too, and he can feel it. He used to give commentary that way. As if everything that happened on the pitch was happening to him.

HASEENA   Well, you never know.

HASAN   No, I know. I know. It can never happen. Tony died a few years ago. When *bhai* told me, I cried. I cried that Tony left like that. He left me. His voice left me.

HASEENA   And now you're leaving me.

HASAN   Hah?

HASEENA   I'm so confused.

HASAN   About what?

HASEENA   *To herself,* You're not educated, you have no money, you smell of chicken . . .

HASAN   You don't sound confused . . .

HASEENA   Can't you understand what I'm saying?

HASAN   If you just explained it to me nicely, instead of
           insulting me . . .

HASEENA   *A bit exasperated,* Do you know what a
           googly is?

HASAN   Don't be stupid. I mean, of course I know. I'm
           a cricketer.

HASEENA   Explain a googly to me.

HASAN   It's when you think the ball is going to turn this
           way, but it turns the other way.

HASEENA   And then?

HASAN   Then what? Then you get bowled.

HASEENA   Yes. Clean bowled.

HASAN   So? *Beat.* Oh. *Oh.* I see. *Chest swelling,* You
           thought I was charm-less. Turns out I am
           charm-ing. And you thought I'll be stuck here
           all my life, but now *I'm* leaving and *you're* stuck
           here! Your college is only ten minutes away.
           How about that, doctor? You know, up until a
           couple of years ago, I used to find you so irritat-
           ing. You looked so odd and all your features
           were topsy-turvy, but suddenly

everything—your eyes, ears, nose, lips, *everything*, has just fallen into place.

HASEENA   Er . . . thank you?

HASAN   Welcome, welcome.

HASEENA   Hasan, you'll go there for one season. Then what?

HASAN   What do you mean?

HASEENA   Even if you score a hundred in every game, you'll still have to come back.

HASAN   You don't know that.

HASEENA   Even if you do, you won't be able to cut chickens anymore.

HASAN   Why not?

HASEENA   You haven't thought this through. You've never left Dongri, Hasan. Now you'll see the world. I don't want you to . . .

HASAN   Hate what I do even more?

HASEENA   Yes.

HASAN   I hate it anyway. I have to prove myself.

HASEENA	No, you don't.
HASAN	To you. I'm going to Canada for you. For us. I will go there and whack the ball around, until the green grass turns blue, until the blue water turns red because I will hit the red cricket ball into the water so many times the colour will run, and it will land on a dolphin's head!
HASEENA	That would kill the dolphin, Hasan.
HASAN	But you are a doctor, so what's the worry?

They both enjoy a moment of silence — take in the fact that they have finally admitted their feelings for one another.

	Haseena . . . if I'm gone for a while, will you . . . wait?
HASEENA	Of course . . .
HASAN	I mean, will you . . . will you . . .
HASEENA	Will I what?
HASAN	Will you give your first kiss to somebody else?
HASEENA	My first kiss? Oh. Hasan, I'm really sorry but . . .

HASAN	But what?
HASEENA	My first kiss has already been given.
HASAN	What? What?
HASEENA	To you.
HASAN	Me?
HASEENA	Yes, you. From the window. I blew you a kiss this morning. When you weren't looking.
HASAN	And I thought that was a fly on my cheek.
HASEENA	Don't act smart.
HASAN	No, no, it was a *flying* kiss, get it? Okay, okay, don't get upset. I'm just nervous.
HASEENA	Don't worry, I'll wait.
HASAN	But why wait? Come to the airport to drop me. I go separately. You go separately. Meet me there. In the crowd, we can hug like we are saying goodbye. And there I can . . .

They both are blushing. Suddenly they turn away from each other at the same time, painfully shy.

Suddenly I don't feel like going anywhere. Forget

cricket. Forget Canada. You be my doctor, and I'll be your patient, Haseena, because I am sick at the thought of leaving you.

The rude beep of a motorcycle horn. They both break out of their trance.

HASEENA   It's Mehndi again. I've told him I don't —

HASAN   Has he been bothering you?

HASEENA   No, no, it's okay . . . he just wants to take me for a ride.

HASAN   Do you want to go?

HASEENA   No, of course not.

HASAN   Then he should respect your decision.

Mehndi honks again.

HASAN   Enough of this.

HASEENA   Just leave it.

HASAN   No, I made a mistake the last time by not standing up for you.

HASEENA   It wasn't a mistake.

HASAN	You're mine now. *To Mehndi,* Listen, Mehndi. Leave her alone. You will treat her with respect! Do you understand?
HASEENA	Hasan, take it easy . . .
HASAN	*To Mehndi,* People fear you but they don't respect you. You need to earn her respect!
HASEENA	That's enough.
HASAN	No, let me get it right this time!
HASEENA	He's not someone you mess with!
HASAN	You think I'm scared of him? *To Mehndi,* I am not scared of you! You will leave Haseena alone! Leave her alone or I'll . . .
HASEENA	Hasan, go easy . . .
HASAN	If you ever bother her again, I'll . . .

He takes his large knife but doesn't know what to do with it. He just waves it around.

I'll show you!

He realizes that he has made a huge mistake. The fear kicks in but he continues to stand his ground.

3.

Two weeks later. Late morning.

The locker room.

Randy enters.

RANDY   Pad up, guys! We've won the toss!

Sam and Ram start padding up.

Sam, I'm sending you lower down the order
today.

SAM   Oh.

RANDY   Our club president will open with Ram. He's
out there warming up, having a smoke. He'll be
in soon. *To Ram,* Just make sure you play out
the first ten-overs. I don't care how many runs
you make, just don't get out.

SAM   You said that to me as well and now I'm
demoted.

RANDY   Look, this team is full of Aussies. They're old,
but don't be fooled. I've played these guys
before. They'll amble up to the wicket and
swing the ball like a pendulum. So just wait till
the shine wears off.

RAM   Oh, fuck.

RANDY   What's wrong?

RAM   I forgot my ball guard.

RANDY   Did you give it to the Russian as a souvenir?

RAM   I need to borrow a ball guard.

           *Everyone suddenly busies themselves doing
           something.*

           Come on, guys.

RANDY   I am *not* sharing a testicle protector with you.

RAM   But I can't go out there without it. That's suicide.

RANDY   You could have syphilis.

RAM   Russian *writers* got syphilis. A century ago.

RANDY   From Russian hookers!

RAM   *To Sam,* Come on, bro.

SAM   Sorry, man. I can't. It's a cultural thing.

RAM   What?

SAM   In China, we don't share ball guards.

RAM   What the hell are you talking about?

SAM   Sorry, but I have a date tonight.

RAM   What's that got to do with anything?

RANDY   You have a date?

SAM   Yes, sir, I do.

RANDY   Shocker.

RAM   Hey, you know what he did once? He really
            liked this girl but he needed a line, you know,
            so he went to her and said, "Listen, I *know*
            Victoria's Secret."

SAM   I thought it was witty, okay?

ABDUL   Victoria Secret?

RAM   It's a lingerie store, bro. It's like a magic cave.
            Women go in there and disappear for weeks.
            Then they come out totally transformed. It's
            amazing. It's like Gandalf's sitting in there with
            a magic wand in one hand and a thong in the
            other. What the hell am I doing? Guys, I need
            a ball guard!

RANDY	For fuck's sake, here! But wear it *outside* your underwear. I don't want any skin contact.
RAM	Thanks, bro. My future children are grateful to you.
RANDY	Doc, you need to pad up too. You're going one down. *Beat.* Okay, Doc?

Doc nods.

He wants to say something but hesitates. Then decides to say it anyway.

DOC	I'd like to say something. *Beat.* Today's my last day with this club.
RAM	You're leaving the club?
DOC	In light of recent events, I have no choice. It would be the right thing to do.
RANDY	The right thing to do would be to stay. To sort things out.
DOC	I am *not* in agreement about bringing Hasan here.
RANDY	You were the only one.
DOC	Which is why I'm the only one who's leaving.

RANDY   This is cricket. We're a team. We can sort
          anything out. Go out there, the two of you,
          bat together, score some runs, and —

DOC   And then what? Have a beer?

RANDY   Have ten beers.

DOC   You think it's that simple?

RANDY   It's that simple. Or at least it should be.

DOC   Well, it's not.

RANDY   Why did you come to this country then? What
          did you decide to bring with you? Your skills as
          a surgeon, or your hate?

DOC   It's not hate.

RANDY   I only see hate, man. That's all I see.

DOC   What is Canada to you? Some sort of safety net
          that you land on, after you've been pushed off a
          cliff?

RANDY   No one was pushed off, Doc. My family came
          here for me. To give me a better education. Only
          they didn't know what to expect. It was a long
          time ago. I can hate too, if I want to.

DOC   So what you're saying is I can't speak the truth.
                 Or I can speak the truth as long as it's palatable.

RAM   What the fuck are you talking about, bro?

DOC   Boy, don't forget your place. We may be in a
                 locker room, but I am *not* your "bro."

RANDY   So as long as he's a bigot, he's your bro?

DOC   The kids in school were right when they called
                 you a whore. You *are* a fucking sellout.

RANDY   How the fuck did they let you into this country,
                 man? I hope that's not what you're teaching
                 your kids. Fuck . . .

DOC   What did you say?

RANDY   Nothing. Let's just get this over with. Go out
                 there and bat.

DOC   Don't ever speak about my kids. You know
                 nothing about my kids.

RANDY   Okay, man. Whatever.

DOC   You know nothing about my son. Nothing.

RANDY   Hey man, calm down.

DOC   I'm not "man." I'm a doctor. I'm —

RANDY   In here, you're just a guy who goes one down.

ABDUL   I feel bad . . . Abdul feel bad . . . I go . . . Doc,
             you stay in team, I tell Hasan no come . . .

DOC   You think that's going to make a difference?
             You leaving? Your brother staying? Will that
             change anything for my son? Hah? Will it? Tell
             me, Abdul . . . are you circumcised?

             Abdul is shocked.

             Answer the question. Are you circumcised? I'll
             bet you are.

RANDY   You're crossing the line, Doc.

DOC   *I'm* crossing the line? *I'm* crossing the line? I'll
             tell you what crossing the line is. During the
             riots, my son and I were stopped by a mob. They
             wanted to know if we were Muslim. They said
             we *looked* Muslim. *Tum Muslim lagte ho, Hindu
             Nahi!* I said we were neither Hindu nor Muslim.
             We're Zoroastrian. So they made us strip. I
             begged them. *Mera beta sirf aath saal ka hai* . . .
             They stripped me first. I'm not circumcised. But
             my son — I started reciting my prayers, I spoke
             in my language and they believed me. But my
             son, when they asked him to speak, he was

             ––––
             111

terrified, he saw men with sticks and knives. How can an eight-year-old speak? You are protecting a Muslim kid, they said. *I'd* had him circumcised! For health reasons. Isn't that just brilliant?

Doc can't go on. Everyone has been stunned into silence. Except Abdul.

ABDUL   But Hindus kill your son. Your son killed by Hindus. What have to do with *me*?

DOC   They thought he was *you*.

4.

The chicken centre. Night. A few hours before Hasan's flight.

The place is closed for business, but Hasan is cleaning up, getting things in shape before he leaves.

HASAN   Remember, Baba, next Sunday. Big order from Ghulam Ali. He wants ten chickens. He's throwing a party for his brother who is being released from jail.

BABA   Yes, yes . . .

HASAN   And before the new stock comes, get the cage
         washed. It's smelling.

BABA   So *janaab* is now giving *me* orders?

HASAN   I'm just fulfilling my duties. As a good
         employee.

BABA   Suddenly become conscientious when you're
         leaving?

HASAN   Baba, you'll miss me, won't you?

BABA   Let me think. No.

HASAN   You'll miss me.

BABA   I know who *won't* miss you.

HASAN   Haseena will surely miss me.

BABA   I doubt she'll even think of you. You're like gas.
         You'll pass.

HASAN   Then why is she coming to say goodbye?

BABA   At this hour?

HASAN   Relax. Her father has just left for his village, and
         her mother and granny snore louder than
         buffalos. They won't notice.

BABA	Well, anyway. You are like a brother to her. Nothing more.
HASAN	That train has passed. And I've got something for her to prove it.
BABA	What?
HASAN	Flowers.
BABA	Flowers?
HASAN	Roses. She likes tulips, but those I could not find here.
BABA	What do you know about tulips?
HASAN	Quite a bit. You're not the only one with culture. But for now, a dozen roses will do.
BABA	A dozen? Where did you get a dozen from?
HASAN	From the graveyard. There's so many bouquets there.
BABA	Yes, cultured indeed.
HASAN	She won't care where I got them from. When you love someone, the intention is all that counts. So I'm going to tell her. Straight up. Like it is.

BABA   Sure, sure.

              Haseena enters carrying a box. Before even
              greeting her, Hasan tells her about the roses
              straight off.

HASAN   I've got something for you. But it's from a
              graveyard.

HASEENA   What?

HASAN   No, no, what I mean is . . . they're roses. It's just
              that they're —

HASEENA   From somebody's grave?

HASAN   Yes.

HASEENA   That's so weird.

BABA   Intention, hah?

HASAN   I was just teasing you. Would I steal roses from
              a graveyard?

              He throws the roses to the ground, pretends that
              Haseena didn't see them.

BABA   You have so much to learn about women.

Then Baba buries his face in the paper but peeks over it as Hasan and Haseena speak in soft tones.

HASAN   I'm sorry. I just wanted to get you something. I have to save money for the taxi to the airport. It's five hundred rupees.

HASEENA   I can't accept those flowers.

               Hasan is disappointed.

               My mother will ask, no? If she sees? I haven't told her anything. As it is, she was so upset about Mehndi. She made my father speak to his father. He will leave me alone now. His father must have given him the thrashing of his life.

HASAN   And a haircut. He needs a thrashing and a haircut. *Beat.* So . . . I'll send you pictures. Of tulips and me staring at the steam clock.

HASEENA   What if you like somebody there?

HASAN   You mean like a girl?

HASEENA   No, no, I mean a cow or buffalo.

HASAN   I can't like anyone. To like someone you need a heart. And I will be leaving mine behind.

BABA   You are pathetic.

HASAN	Can you just—
BABA	Sorry.
HASAN	*Softer,* Haseena, there is one more thing I want to give . . . but you'll have to imagine it, okay? Just imagine these hands, okay. Not covered in blood, but clean, totally clean. Then just imagine this apron, not covered in blood, but—
HASEENA	I get it. No blood.
HASAN	Now imagine these arms . . . I am close to you, standing only inches from you, and these arms they just circle around you, as though I am circling the world, because you are the world to me, Haseena, you are the world to me. Can you imagine that?
HASEENA	Always.
HASAN	I will hug my cricket bat tighter, but you are a close second.
HASEENA	You are an idiot. But you're my idiot.
HASAN	I would rather be your idiot than another woman's wise man.
BABA	That actually made sense.

Both Hasan and Haseena, together.

TOGETHER   Baba!

HASAN   Take care, my . . . friend. *He whispers,* Airport
              tonight. See you there.

HASEENA   Even I got something for you. But you can use it
              only once you're back.

              *She hands him a small box. He opens it. In it is a
              small handheld battery-operated fan.*

              He turns it on.

HASAN   My fan . . .

              *It starts whirring a beautiful Haseena breeze into
              his face. He revels in it. But, as always, Baba butts
              in and takes the fan away from him.*

BABA   *Huzur,* aren't you forgetting something?

HASAN   What?

BABA   The card. You didn't give her the card.

HASEENA   What card?

HASAN   *Alarmed, annoyed,* What card?

BABA   Don't you think she needs to see it?

HASAN   *Sternly,* No, not really.

HASEENA   Why not?

HASAN   Because there is no card.

            *Baba pulls a card out from his pocket. Hasan
            immediately snatches it from him. Hasan wants
            to pulverize Baba but he cannot show it. He turns
            to Haseena full of grace.*

            You see, the thing is, as you know, immigration
            laws are very complex. They are extremely com-
            plex things, very nuanced, and sometimes —

BABA   Hasan, you have a plane to catch.

HASAN   Yes, so, in order to get the tourist visa, I had to
            prove to them, convince the authorities, that I
            have a solid reason for coming back. So I had to
            make a card, you see, to convince the powers
            that be that I will not stay back in Canada.

HASEENA   What card?

HASAN   It's hard to describe. It's like a birthday card, but
            more serious.

BABA   It's a wedding card.

HASAN   Yes, yes, that would be quite accurate. It's an
             invitation to our wedding.

HASEENA   *What?*

HASAN   Relax, it's just to prove that I have a beautiful
             bride waiting for me, and all of Canada is not
             enough to keep me away from her.

HASEENA   How dare you?

BABA   That's what I said.

HASAN   It was your idea!

BABA   *Softly to Hasan,* An idea is something good. This
             is bad, so bad.

HASEENA   You did not even bother to ask me?

HASAN   But it's fake. It's not even real. It's so stupid.

HASEENA   Our wedding is stupid?

             *Like a character in a cartoon strip, Baba slowly
             tip toes away.*

HASAN   No, of course not. I had to do this . . .

             *He looks pleadingly towards Haseena, but she is
             silent.*

There was no other way . . .

She is still silent.

Your silence is scaring me.

After a sterner silence.

HASEENA   It's okay.

HASAN   What?

HASEENA   It's okay. I understand.

HASAN   You do?

HASEENA   Yes. There's something I need to tell you. I have to be honest with you.

HASAN   Anything, you can tell me anything.

HASEENA   *I was the one who went to Mehndi for help.* He did not come to me. I went to him first.

HASAN   What are you talking about?

HASEENA   I study hard, Hasan. Very hard. My marks are good. But I don't know if I have what it takes to get into the best college. The competition is fierce. The cut-off is too high. So I went to Mehndi.

HASAN   For what?

HASEENA   He knows people . . . who know people . . . how
           to get high marks. He said he would get me a
           mark sheet with very high marks. Just in case
           I don't do as well as I need to. In exchange, he
           said I would have to go for a ride on his bike
           with him. Which I did. Once. But then he went
           mad, he wouldn't leave me alone. That's why he
           is behaving this way. It's not his fault. The fault
           is mine.

HASAN   How could you?

HASEENA   You made a fake card. I made a fake mark sheet.
           We both did what we had to do.

HASAN   It's not the same thing.

HASEENA   Maybe. Maybe what I did is worse. But I did it.
           And I stand by it.

           They both think about what has just transpired.

           I know you are disappointed in me.

HASAN   I'm not disappointed. I'm scared.

HASEENA   Why?

HASAN   Because . . . because you hid it from me so well.

I couldn't see it. And it makes me wonder what else you are hiding.

HASEENA   I want more from life. And if I don't get it, I will not be okay. But you don't want much. Cricket is enough for you.

HASAN   *You* are enough for me.

HASEENA   Do you remember my sister, Rubina?

HASAN   Kind of.

HASEENA   She left Dongri ten years ago. She got married to the man she loved. They live in the suburbs in a one bedroom flat with three children. They watch movies every Sunday. That's not the life I want.

HASAN   Then what? What do you want?

HASEENA   I want you to want more. Show me you want more.

HASAN   All I know is that I can't live without you. Can you live without me?

Haseena looks around.

HASAN   What are you doing?

HASEENA	Checking.
HASAN	For what?
HASEENA	Eyes.
HASAN	Eyes?

She takes on last look around the place. No one is around. She gives Hasan a kiss on the cheek.

He is stunned.

HASEENA   Say something.

He kisses her on the cheek.

Well said. Goodbye, Hasan. Come back soon.

She leaves.

HASAN   *Delirious,* Fuck Canada. Fuck cricket. Fuck the world. What the fuck . . .

5.

The locker room. Same day. Late evening. After the game.

From offstage, we hear shouts of "West Coast!

West Coast!"—a victorious battle cry from the team.

We hear Sam say, "I am a batting machine!"

They enter—raucous, full of joy.

Randy opens an ice box. Everyone grabs a beer except Doc and Abdul.

Everyone is upbeat, except Doc, who is less energetic but has a quiet peace to him.

RANDY   That was a great game, boys! Great game! Where's the rest of the team?

RAM   Rubbing defeat into the opposition's noses. Our club president smoked a cigar in their captain's face! I love it! A cigar! Hey Abdul, I don't think we need your brother anymore!

RANDY   Yes, give me my money back.

SAM   Yeah, we revoke our offer!

RANDY   While we're at it, let's send Abdul back too! You illegal prick!

RAM   Whoa, that's pushing it, man. That's insensitive. But then again, we're champions, so who cares?

SAM   Yeah, we can say anything, can't we?

RAM   Hell, yeah!

SAM   *To Ram,* That was a rhetorical question, you
        dumb fuck! Don't you understand tone?

        *Someone's phone starts ringing. It's a bit muffled.
        Coming from someone's bag.*

RANDY   Well done, Sam!

SAM   I'm taking everyone to China with me!

RAM   What have *you* eaten today?

SAM   *Indicating Randy,* Not *his* food!

        *Randy goes for Sam with his bat. Sam is shit
        scared.*

RANDY   Hey, not my food, okay? I'm serious. I'll fuck
        you up.

        But then—

        Ha ha! I got you!

        *The phone keeps ringing. Abdul senses it's his. By
        the time he recovers it from his bag, it's stopped.*

SAM   You're such a weird captain.

RANDY   Okay, guys! I just want to acknowledge one per-
        formance today. A standout performance. Doc,
        you played like a champ.

        *Doc acknowledges the compliment. The boys raise
        their beers to Doc.*

        *Abdul picks up a beer from the cooler and offers it
        to Doc. From a distance. But very hesitantly,
        humbly.*

ABDUL   Like true champ.

        *But Doc just waves his hand. No. Abdul drinks
        instead.*

RANDY   Fuck, I thought you didn't touch alcohol. Isn't it
        against your religion?

ABDUL   I not touching. Going directly inside body.

SAM   So Abdul, how much did you score today?
        Come on, superstar. Tell us how much you
        scored.

ABDUL   You know . . . everyone know . . .

SAM   But why don't you tell us? Maybe we forgot.

His phone rings again. This time he answers.

ABDUL   It's Baba!

SAM   Answer the question!

ABDUL   Duck, okay? Zero.

SAM   That's right, brother. First ball. Out first ball.
             Even *I*, worst player on the team, scored more!
             Quack, quack, quack . . .

ABDUL   *Into phone,* What?

             *He signals for everyone to be quiet. But the boys
             are raucous.*

             *Ram imitates the way Abdul left the ball in the
             game, a total misjudgement, which left his stump
             reeling.*

RAM   The stump flew a mile!

SAM   Yeah, I hope your brother has better judgement
             than you, man!

RAM   *To Abdul,* You are blind as a *bat!*

SAM   Batman!

But Abdul isn't listening. His phone falls to the ground.

ABDUL   No . . . no . . . no . . .

He sits down on a bench. He puts his head in his hands. They all go quiet.

RANDY   Abdul?

ABDUL   They killed him.

RANDY   What? Who?

ABDUL   He liked girl . . . on way to airport . . . they killed my Hasan.

Everyone just stands and watches as Abdul crumbles.

6.

The chicken centre. Dawn.

Baba is alone. He is closing the shop for the day. Or the week.

He can barely move. He covers the chicken cage with a black cloth.

When he is almost done, he sees something on the counter. It is Hasan's small fan. In a daze, he turns it on.

And breaks down.

7.

The locker room.

The boys are gathered, still dealing with the aftershock of the news.

Randy takes the photograph of Hasan that Abdul showed him earlier and pastes it on the wall.

Doc gets up, places his cricket bat under the photograph, and leans it against the wall as a mark of respect.

Others follow. One by one, they place their bats for Hasan.

Lights leave the players as we hear the commentary of Tony Greig. It is a montage of some of Tony's most ebullient commentary.

TONY GREIG "This is his first ball, through the gap on the off side, just listen to it. Oh, well played, that's four, a lovely, elegant cover drive. Oh, he's hit this one miles! Great shot! Oh, it's a biggie! Straight over the top! The little man has hit the big fella for six! He's half his size and he's smashed him down the ground. Whadda player! Whadda wonderful player! Oh, this is high, what a six, what a six, it's on the roof, there it is! They're dancing in the aisles in Sharjah . . ."

Lights fade.

END OF PLAY.

Acknowledgements

The playwright is grateful to the following individuals for their help during the development of this play: Sanjay Talwar, Nadeem Philip, Risha Nanda, Shekhar Paleja, Munish Sharma, Raugi Yu, Anousha Alamian, Parm Soor, Kamyar Pazandeh, David Adams, Carlen Escarraga, Pippa Mackie, Richard Newman, Zahf Paroo, Eva Barrie, Sam Khalileh, Isaac Thomas, Sugith Varughese, Simu Liu, Majdi Bou-Matar, Shelly Antony, Jake Runeckles, Gabe Grey, Cyrus Faird, Miquelon Rodriguez, Supinder Vraich, and Bilal Baig.

To the Canada Council for the Arts and the British Columbia Arts Council for their generous and timely support.

And a special thank you to Bill Millerd, Rachel Ditor, Nina Lee Aquino, Philip Akin, Matt McGeachy, Stephanie Hargreaves, Gavan Cheema, Veronique West, and Boman Irani.

ANOSH IRANI has published four critically acclaimed novels: *The Cripple and His Talismans*, a national bestseller; *The Song of Kahunsha*, which was an international bestseller and was a finalist for Canada Reads and the Ethel Wilson Fiction Prize; *Dahanu Road*, which was nominated for the Man Asian Literary Prize; and *The Parcel*, a finalist for the Governor General's Literary Award, the Rogers Writers' Trust Fiction Prize, and the Ethel Wilson Fiction Prize. It was longlisted for the DSC Prize for South Asian Literature and the International Dublin Literary Award. *The Parcel* was chosen as one of the Best Books of the Year by the *Globe and Mail*, *Quill & Quire*, *National Post*, CBC Books, and *The Walrus*. His play *Bombay Black* won five Dora Mavor Moore Awards, including for Outstanding New Play, and his anthology, *The Bombay Plays: The Matka King & Bombay Black*, was a finalist for the Governor General's Literary Award. *The Men in White* was nominated for three Jessie Richardson Awards, including for Outstanding Original Script. His work has been translated into eleven languages.